Log Book

Frank Laskier

Solis Press

ALSO BY FRANK LASKIER
AND AVAILABLE FROM SOLIS PRESS:

My Name is Frank
Unseen Harbour

TO DESFARGES

WITHOUT WHOSE FRIENDSHIP

I SHOULD NEVER HAVE WRITTEN THIS BOOK

Originally published in 1942 by George Allen & Unwin, London.
This edition completely reset with minor spelling changes and some
archaic language removed. A new introduction has been added.

Caution: this book contains words and views that are offensive and
upsetting. The book was first published in 1942 when such attitudes
and language were not challenged.

Published in 2021 by Solis Press

Typographical arrangement and introduction copyright
© 2021 Solis Press

Cover image: based on the original jacket design of the 1942 edition

All rights reserved. No part of this publication may be reproduced,
stored in a retrieval system, or transmitted, in any form or by any
means, electronic, mechanical, photocopying, recording or otherwise,
except as permitted by the UK Copyright, Designs and Patents Act
1988, without the prior permission of the publisher.

This book is sold subject to the condition that it shall not, by way or
trade or otherwise, be lent, resold, hired out or otherwise circulated
without the publisher's prior consent in any form of binding or cover
other than in which it is published and without a similar condition
including this condition being imposed on the subsequent purchaser.

ISBN: 978-1-910146-48-4

Published by Solis Press, Tunbridge Wells, Kent, England

Web: www.solispress.com | *Twitter*: @SolisPress

Introduction to this new edition

*L*OG BOOK, ORIGINALLY PUBLISHED in 1942, tells the story of a merchant seaman's life on the oceans, from green novice to war veteran. Despite being described as a work of fiction, the main character, Jack, is a thinly veiled portrait of the author himself, Frank Laskier.

Laskier had shot to fame through a series of radio broadcasts where he described in graphic and terrifying detail what it was like to serve on the convoys bringing vital supplies across the oceans into Britain during the Second World War. Listeners were astounded yet fascinated by the voice of an ordinary man describing the horrific realities of the war at sea. Overnight Laskier became a hero and a poster-boy for the merchant navy, a maritime institution often overlooked by the Royal Navy's more glamorous image.

In *Log Book*, Laskier tells the story of a boy who lies about his age to follow his dream of becoming a merchant seaman, a dream inspired not only by the many sailors within his own family and community but also by the romantic tales of his literary heroes, Joseph Conrad and John Masefield. However, it is a hard life and Jack battles with himself and his strict moral upbringing as he tries to resist the temptations of drink and women on offer at every port. Eventually, he succumbs and finds himself on a path that nearly destroys him as he loses the girl he loves, is sent to prison and suffers numerous injuries as a result of his violent and aggressive temper. In time, Jack manages to pull his life together, only to be confronted by the atrocities of war.

As Jack witnesses the suffering and loss of close family and friends, the tragic aftermath of a sinking of a British ship carrying evacuated children to safety in North America, he is driven by revenge. He rails against those on the home front who squander the petrol and supplies brought in from the convoys at such a cost to him and his fellow mariners. Yet, he is touched by the kindness of strangers as he takes shelter from the air raids. The emotional charge of these very raw accounts still rings true today as many battle with post-traumatic stress disorder, a condition that was barely recognised at the time.

Log Book

THERE HAD NEVER BEEN such a snowfall. In the minds of the oldest inhabitants no memory could be found of such cold, bitter weather. People forced to work, went out with three pairs of socks, army boots, sweaters and balaclava helmets. Business men went to offices looking like watchkeepers on destroyers, muffled to the eyes and ears with thick wool. At home housewives left sculleries piled with dirty dishes, floors unswept, and cowered over fires. Half the heat went up the chimney—wasted, as was half their talk.

The wind, cold and venomous, arose from the depths of the Arctic—swept over Norway, down across the North Sea—ripped and tore down the counties of Scotland and England. Tiny boats at anchorage tossed and curveted at their moorings. Seagulls moaned over the waters. They hovered over ships—in long glides they swept around the stern and alighted on the waters, waiting for food to be flung to them. The cook, toiling and sweating, would stagger to the rail and empty the bucket of slops over the side. Screaming the gulls rose, flapping over the waters—they circled aimlessly around and then dived for the food which lay greasily on the surface. Before they could check to collect it, the wind, with the apologetic moan of a moneylender before foreclosure, swept them away. The food sank, and the seagulls, fighting among themselves, looked for it in vain.

The wind careered on, swept over a little huddle of cottages on the river bank, tore up a street, and was promptly sucked down the chimney of a house. Down past the bricks, the soot, and into the fire—blowing out the flames—pouring smoke and dust into the room. For a few seconds the fire became dull and heavy, the room clouded with smoke. Then, as the wind passed on, the room cleared.

It was a room in an old house on a little side street that ran down to the sea. At the bottom of the street was an old stone promenade and a pier which, in summer, was crowded with trippers but was now a long deserted waste. The houses had been built about one hundred and fifty years ago, and had been for the almost exclusive use of the fisherfolk. The local lifeboat lay at the bottom of the street, and the crew lived around about.

The number of the house was fifty-seven. It was small and dark, and packed with memories of the people who lived there. The parents had moved into the house when they had first married; their children had been born in the little upper room. Eleven children—six boys and five girls. One of the little girls, at the age of nine, had been laid dead on the parlour table. Three of the elder boys had done their courting in the room—so had the girls. On the wall was an old grandmother clock, and the father's medical discharge from the last war. A photograph of the youngest son, in the blue of the Royal Navy, helped to clutter up a crowded, dusty mantelpiece. A tiny scullery at the back, spotlessly neat and clean. The lavatory was at the bottom of the yard—a yard that had once been full of driftwood that the children collected from the shore. A tiny hole in the ceiling of the back bedroom marked the passage of an incendiary bomb. It was an old family; clean living and honourable. At the top of the road was the school. Further on was the church. The room was full of comfortable, warm furniture, a wireless set, and stacks of books.

Before the fire sat two people. One was a mother—old, fat and comfortable; and her son—still young, in his twenties; very sleepy, awakened from his dreams. Both of them started. The mother coughed—the man stared into the fire and continued his dreams. He was home, a sailor. The war had taken him, lifted him, made him, and then shattered him. With a feeling of bewilderment he stared at two crutches leaning against the opposite wall. Reflectively he scratched a useless stump—small, grotesque. Reflectively he stared at what had once been his right leg.

His mother's voice, full of love and understanding, came to him across the room. "There was a man called for you this afternoon, Jack. Said he was some sort of a reporter. He's calling back to-night." Her son sat on before the fire and brooded.

St. James's Church was very new but looked quite old. All the best people attended. Sunday evening service was favoured amongst them, and there they met—dressed as neatly and as comfortably as they could arrange—worshipping the God who, with a forbearance no one could appreciate, admitted them to live, love and fulfil their destinies. Prompt at six o'clock the church would be full. The high nave, dim and foggy, would be filled with the quiet rustle of Sunday clothes, the murmur of the vergers and the gentle whisper of the organ. The glory of the stained-glass windows was lost with the light that had faded outside. The voice of the organ died and vanished as the voice of the vicar, from the open vestry, filled the church. The congregation stood. "Praise ye the Lord"—and in harmony sweet, yet stale with constant usage: "The Lord's name be praised." "Hymn four hundred and twenty-six— Hymn four hundred and twenty-six," called the voice of the vicar. Calm, impersonal and clear. Then the organ pealed out and the choir moved forth—all out of step—shambling into their stalls. Boys in front; cassocked, surpliced, Eton collared. Behind, the men; so dignified, so ethereal, and so utterly sexless. Staunch business men, good living, and in some cases hard bargainers. The boys, like all good choir boys had been driven to church by their parents; the men by their wives—as are all bad tenors, reedy baritones, and passable bass singers.

Leading the boys were five youngsters: Dick, Joe, Tom, Jack and Harry.

Dick really could fight and swim; no thought of danger ever entered his bullet head. Orchards were made to be robbed, windows to be broken, and school for him was just a place to go on rainy days. Far more times than he ever had hot Sunday dinners he was thrashed for playing truant.

Joe was quiet and said little. He was obstinate as a granny knot on a wet night. Never wanting anything important, he always pleased himself. He went fishing in his father's boat at fourteen. The sea claimed him—his ambition vanished. Poor Joe.

Tom, Jack's best friend, was a small, rather heavily built boy; grey-eyed, black haired, and of a quiet nature. He was of the type that always manages to gain an ascendancy over weaker people; seemingly has the power to get on—to push forward—yet never really does. All that these two boys possessed of dreams or property, they shared. Tom was as honest as the daylight, and as gentle. Nothing ever disturbed or shook him—ever shook his sane, ordered view of life. Even at the tender age, and it is a tender age, of fourteen.

Jack was as vivid and imaginative as Tom was solid. They fought common enemies, and dreamed of their future together. They would go to sea.

Harry tagged on to the coat tails of the others and provided a Greek chorus of sorrow whichever way their diverse fortunes took them.

One Sunday Jack was disfigured by a large black eye, as was George Smith, another choir boy. Master Smith, through the delay caused by having to wash his face and get a more presentable appearance was too late for choir and attended the service from the congregation—snivelling audibly. The victory, a technical one, had been given to Jack; though it had consisted in Jack receiving only a slightly less severe beating than Mr. Smith.

Jack was a dark boy, tall for his years, an insignificant member of a large family. And he was already a problem for his parents. With a father who was an ex-sailor, and a mother who was wife, daughter, and mother of sailors to deter him, he still longed for the sea. A battle, silent, unresting, went on continually in their small home. Jack lost. Do you remember those past defeats in your own home? Jack lost.

The boys left school and choir for the world. Dick went to sea, and kept at sea. Joe went into his father's fishing boat. Tom drifted down to the dockyard, and was away in the twinkling of an eye on a banana boat. Harry was indentured as an apprentice to a tanker firm. Jack went with his father, to work in his laundry as a van boy, collecting dirty linen. Collecting dirty linen and listening to the complaints of housewives. "For the fifth time, where are my husband's two collars?" Taking the clean laundry back. "What's this, two and ninepence? Far too much." A stream of complaints. There, in all its dreadful monotony, was the job. Yet Jack's father was one of the gentlest and most intelligent of men, his one thought was to see that his sons were as well placed in life as was possible—and this son was to learn the business.

Jack planned and schemed to get away to sea. His reading didn't help him to settle down. *The Magnet, Boys' Own Paper,* then thrillers, and so to Wodehouse. Always reading of money, of people who had so much of it that it never entered their consciousness to worry about it. Not good reading when the reader was continually pestered about two-and-ninepenny laundry bills.

Then one day came Conrad and Masefield. In them Jack found all he had longed for—the call of the sea. And he listened. He listened to such effect that he ran away. Running away to sea presented different scenes, different people.

Imagine a boy—roughly treated, perhaps beaten, rushing from his home and hearth to tramp the hills—tramp the hills to a seaport! There to be welcomed aboard by the Jolly Tars! And thence—straight to the Spanish Main!

Jack's departure was far more ordinary. Sent one day by a trusting parent to take laundry to a ship, he went aboard as ordered, took the money from the chief officer and surrendered to that august being his parcel of clean shirts. Down the gangway, picking his way over railway lines, he passed another ship in dry dock. The dockyard gang was taking the baulks of timber from the ship's side as the dock filled with water. The gangway hovered loose and flappy, ready to be swung up and inboard. As he passed this entrancing scene, Jack looked up. A large man, red-faced and beery, looked down. The man shouted; "Hey you, do you want a trip to Australia? You do? Well, come on up!"

The interview, like all important meetings, was short and sweet. Jack swore he was eighteen—had neither mother nor father, and had done one trip before. He was signed on. When he went outside to the lower bridge the whistle was blowing and the gangway was up. His sea career had started with six and threepence halfpenny of stolen money, the clothes he stood up in, and a boundless faith.

Jack was full of his own importance, impudent, and very stupid. He was not sea sick, of which he was very proud. But he didn't like the idea of scrubbing mess rooms, cleaning the bosun's room, and generally acting as ship's scivvy. In any case, he saw no reason why he should do these things properly. Naturally the bosun's anger was aroused—and a bosun's anger is not a nice thing to arouse! The deck-boy was told off to work below; to scrub and re-scrub the fo'castle. This to him seemed an injustice, a foul trick; persecution in fact. He wended his indignant way to the bridge to tell the captain. Half-way up he was met by the stand-by man—lugged back aft—and it needs no enlargement on my part to tell what happened. The whole truth came out. Jack deserved all he got—and he got it.

Gibraltar was passed one early morning, a clean, beautiful sight, with the blue waters of the Straits and the whiteness of a Spanish village on one side.

The temperature went up—and then came prickly heat. This is caused by being dirty—not washing away the sweat from one's clothes and body—and by eating too much. His body was covered

with tiny raised pimples. Mouth white and furry, tongue hideous-
ly coated. Epsom salts by the packet and No. 9 pills by the dozen
were produced. He was dosed to the eyes and excused work. The
deck-boy reader of Conrad and Masefield was publicly called "a
dirty, filthy, lazy little bastard."

Jack went down to the depths of despair and misery until, one
day, it occurred to him that if he kept clean and quiet, and did his
work, his tormentors would leave him alone. So from that day he
retired within himself, and decided that if the glory and heroism
of sea life had died with Conrad, he would dream of it.

It was in this state of mind that he got to Port Said. He was
robbed right and left, and gave one bearded, lecherous scoundrel
ten shillings for four smudged photographs so filthy that they
were funny.

They steamed down the canal in the blazing sunlight and his possessions were increased by two pairs of khaki shorts, one white
shirt, soap, toothpaste and brush, and also three pounds against
his name on the accounts book. And the photographs.

The canal deepened to deep green waters as pilots were changed
at the Bitter Lakes, then narrowed to the entrancing, gleaming,
green ribbon that ran to Suez. The wake of the ship curled and
splashed against the banks, and along the tow-path trudged tiny
Arabs pulling scows loaded with large, fat Arabs. Occasionally a
resplendent figure astride a camel rolled past—a huge rifle swung
at the side in a leather sheath. Camel Corps! Jack leaned over the
rail and gazed avidly. The hoarse shout of the mate cut through
the air: "Where's your topee? … that's twice I've told you. Get up
on the bridge!"

Up on the bridge, in the peace and quiet of his room, the captain read the riot act. The old "I hereby fine and log you the sum
of five shillings" was spoken, and a chastened, very frightened boy
was sent aft—oppressed by the majesty of the law.

Down into the Red Sea, passing Perim, then the glaring search-light of Aden, and so past Ras al-Hadd and into the Persian Gulf. A dreadful monotonous coastline, hideous with huge yellow hills—no sign of life and no green fields. Flying-fish sped in huge shoals over the water, and once was seen the glimmering length of a shark as it hovered, motionless, six feet below the surface.

So on to Abadan—just a line of numbered jetties, a lot of tank-ers, heat, dust, and the greasy, pervading stench of crude oil. Ashore was a company canteen. Books of money tickets were issued—valued three shillings—to each man. No actual money was allowed. Beer was one and ninepence a bottle, but lemonade with an ice in it was only threepence. It is in such a way that all good tanker men keep sober—or are supposed to. There can be no more wonderful sight than that of a huge fireman delicately sipping a soft, iced, pink drink.

A launch took all hands back to the ship at ten o'clock. That night one of the firemen brought aboard two bottles of araqi, a native drink made from date juice. He and his mate drank them-selves through all the stages, beginning with happiness and end-ing with delirious anger. Whilst in the latter state the fireman attacked his mate, beating him to a swollen pulp before being overpowered; then tried to kill himself when he realised what he had done. Jack watched him being put into a straitjacket. He was scared almost out of his wits and swore never to drink.

The ship left Abadan, steamed down the Gulf, then headed down the line to Australia. Three weeks without sight of ship or land. Three weeks of peace, contentment, and the soothing rhythm of life at sea. The sun rose each morning from a cloudless horizon in a blaze of blue and gold.

All of one day Jack had been busy and happy slapping white paint on the rail. No one had told him off, and one man had even joked with him. He had his tea of Irish stew and bread and jam, then, after washing up, went on the fo'castle head and sat down on the bitts. It was getting dark, and the sea was a beautiful black velvet. The sky was a poem of green and gold in the west. The curtain of night—like a coat studded with snowflakes—was gently folding over from the east. A warm, gentle breeze ruffled his hair and soothed the burning sunburn on his face. Over to the right, two little black clouds, like galleons of old, hung motionless, etched against the gold. The white bow wave hissed and caressed the ship's side, and left a wake spotted with phosphorus—beautiful and thrilling—leading back to the dark. Porpoises, leaving green trails of light, sped and darted ahead like ballet dancers, leading the ship in happy escort. Far above in the stillness the look-out hummed "Shenandoah," as the foremast traced long sweeping arcs below the skies. The light fled to its closure as faintly and pathetically as the music of Schumann. And as Jack sat and drank this in with a quiet and a scruffy little soul, he found Conrad, found Masefield—found the boundless peace of his heritage, the sea. He never lost them.

Fremantle, Melbourne, and Sydney were all visited. Nothing happened: except just at Sydney. The carpenter, in a sudden excess of friendliness, lent Jack ten shillings. With the four half-crowns hot in his pocket he went ashore.

The strangeness of his surroundings so scared the boy that he hung about the gates of the oil installation, afraid to let the ship out of his sight. From there he went for a walk around the bay, and found a tiny swimming pool. A stone breakwater kept out the sharks; the grass was green and smooth. Like a young tornado, he dashed back aboard the ship. Stole, or maybe borrowed is a better word, a bathing costume, took some bread and meat from the mess room, and went back to his pool. The heat of the day had traced white runnels of sweat down his thin shanks. With a gasp of joy he dived into the water—clear, salty and refreshing. Nearly all day he swam about in the pool quiet and alone, watching the great ships, with quite a professional eye as they pulled out. Later in the day he sat down on the grass and ate his meal; dreaming of the day when a girl—some beautiful, exquisite, golden-haired girl—would ask him about his job. He would stroke the four golden bars on his sleeve and say, "I'm a ship's captain—that's my craft over there."

But all good things come to an end, and as evening fell he realised he had been adrift all day. Not a stroke had he done—he would land in trouble again. Maybe another terrifying interview with the skipper. Undoubtedly he would be logged. Perhaps a black discharge.

He raced back but no one was on board. The fo'castle was as dirty as only the fo'castle of a ship in port can be dirty. Jack set to work, thinking of the bosun's boot. He scrubbed tables, chairs, and floors; made all the bunks, and tidied the bosun's room. Then grimy, tired, and very near to tears, he sat down dejectedly in a fo'castle smelling of soapy woodwork to await his punishment.

The crowd came back at midnight. They were all drunk. They took no notice of him and were sick all over his nice clean deck. The bosun was adrift for two days and had completely forgotten him.

From Sydney they went to Pulau Sumba, and two days out Jack learned afresh about the sea. He saw death. The sailors were painting ship and the boy was doing some cleaning on the bridge. He watched the bosun as he was hauled up in a chair to the truck of the foremast. Up he went, his bare arms and shoulders silhouetted against the blue sunny sky, his face hard and intent on the job. The little patch of bald on the top of his head gleamed with sweat. Then the sailor below bent the end of the rope around a cleat and waited for bosun to shout "lower and away." Suddenly the chair seemed to disintegrate. Bosun went hurtling down thirty feet to the iron deck. He landed in a soft, huddled heap; there was a thud as his head jerked back and burst on the pipeline. Jack stood and could not move—could not take his eyes from that dreadfully pathetic figure, as he saw it twist and die below him. He suddenly turned and raced like a madman down the ladder—round the midship house—through the centre castle to the forrard deck. Bosun was dead when he got there. Jack stood with chippy, the second mate, and two A.B.s, as the sun beamed down, and the engine chuffed on like a tired old local train.

But for them the world stood still.

In silence, the bosun was lifted up—his body, with its broken back, sagged backwards; his head dripped blood. He was lowered on to a stretcher, and Jack was curtly told by the carpenter to "clean up that mess."

At six that night they buried him. Sewn up in clean, white canvas, his body was laid on the poop deck and covered with the flag. The ship was very still. A man on the bridge tolled the bell— the crew stood around clean and neat. The captain was in full uniform. The spirit of old bosun seemed to fill that little group— hovering over his shattered body. The captain's deep voice read the haunting service for the Burial of the Dead at Sea. "So we commit the body, this our brother, to the deep." He nodded to the bearers and they tilted the hatch-board on which the body rested. There was a scraping noise and bosun slid down. His body turned one pitiful somersault, landed with a thud in the black waters, and vanished. There was the gruff murmur of deep voices as the Lord's Prayer was recited to its splendid end: "For thine is the Kingdom, the Power and the Glory." The setting sun turned each face to sculptured bronze—hard, gnarled hands knotted over each other—clear eyes that knew death as the final end, sometimes as a merciful release; "For ever and ever, Amen." Little Jack went into the dim, shadowy fo'castle and cried as though his heart would break.

For a week afterwards the ship was a nightmare for Jack. He had to clean out the dead man's room before it was locked. That dark door, in the darkest corner of the alleyway, was the home of a ghost. In the quiet of the night he would lie awake—and shiver. After that week, to all but Jack, bosun was forgotten as though he had never been.

Pulau Sumba: blazing hot, full of labouring locals and huge policemen. Jack went ashore, his eyes wide with astonishment and his scrimpy body taut with excitement. Up the road and into the local store. He wasn't robbed—much; he merely paid out English prices for Japanese goods. The boss of the place showed him a place to eat. It was a rather large upper room, spotlessly clean, filled with locals who, to Jack's surprise and joy, wore their shirts outside their trousers, and dug their food from bowls—with spoons— and ate out of the spoons with sticks. Jack was getting a certain amount of sense by this time—he sat and admired, but he used a spoon and fork.

Throughout all this time he had never once written home—why, it is impossible to say. Maybe a psychologist could. …

The next port of call was a tiny little village in the Dutch East Indies. Miles up the river, hidden away from the eyes of inquisitive travellers, a base was being constructed for an ally. He got a tremendous thrill from seeing people who really did live in straw houses perched on sticks in the middle of the stream. Miles above, a huge snow-capped mountain—shading down from black rock and snow to green. A strange, wonderful place, where the boys went ashore and brought back large, hairy heads—which later turned out to be coconuts!

All night long the stand-by man would fish. He leaned over the rail and condescended to talk to the boy. "I was here once before, in a Harrison boat," he said, "and when the boys went ashore for a drink they had to walk two bloody miles through a jungle to get it. On the way back they gets attacked by a flaming big gorilla. They all gets stuck into it and were torn, and scratched, and bleeding.

But they finally gets it down and drags it aboard. They slings it down the lazarette, and they gives it no food for seven days. After that it gets so tame that they signs it on as a trimmer. It used to go below with the boys on the twelve to four, with a sweat-rag round its neck, and growl about the grub." Jack's eyes were as wide as saucers with awe. And he believed that yarn for nearly two trips.

Then the rest of the boys came on board. There was some sort of local poison that they had got on shore, and it was having its effect. Outside, beyond the pool of light over the gangway the stand-by man and Jack could hear a man stumbling along. He seemed to be having a hysterical argument with somebody. It was the donkey-man—still in his engine-room clothes—as he had gone down the gangway for a quick one. His face, as he came under the light, looked blotched, and red and swollen. He stopped at the quay-side and looked up at the ship; a big, grimy figure, gazing up the gangway to the faces of the man and boy—then passing to the outlines of the ship. "You dirty, hungry, lousy bastard! You stinking, bloody old death trap." His voice rose to a scream: "You … you death ship! Hey, boy, call the bosun—and tell him to come ashore and meet the bloody madam." He stood there swaying, and they could see the sweat slowly trickle down his face. Or was it tears—the dead bosun was his brother. The stand-by man stood at the top of the ladder. "Come aboard," he said, "come up now mate and get some kip." The donkey-man looked at him, then he slowly started to crawl up the ladder. Up and up, dragging one foot after the other, his gnarled hands gripping the rail. Up and up, away from the land, away from the whores, and away from himself. In his ascent he was not just Jim, the poor drunk. He was all the Jims, all the sailors. Leaving all the sordidness and filth of the land—leaving that land—crossing that silent, inviting strip of water—stepping into a new world. On board, the ghost of his brother waited to lead him gently to his bunk. His footsteps rang hollowly as he slumped along the darkness of the deck and vanished into the fo'castle.

Then came the second cook—a man of such silent, awful lechery that Jack turned to water every time he looked at him. Up he came, stone sober, with a film of satiety over his eyes. Silently he padded up—great patches of sweat under his arms—to go aft and furtively examine himself.

Then came the skipper, the poor old man. Out of a rackety Packard he stepped. His whites were still white, but very crumpled; his black bootlace of a tie twisted somewhere under his left ear. He came up very quietly, with a curt "goodnight" to the quartermaster. Then he saw Jack. "What the hell's that boy doing up here at this time of night? Get out—turn in—or I'll soon find you a job to do. The boy turned and ran aft; the fo'castle was very quiet and very dim.

Then the boys came in. All drunk, all happy, and all dangerous. An argument started between two of them—about a woman. All became very still as they sat opposite sides of the mess table and argued. One was a Liverpool-Irish stoker, the other an ex-navy man. The language was terrific, and then quietened as one man got up and turned his back. It was a dangerous thing to do. "You liar!" The two men were immediately at each others throats. Men leapt into bunks or crowded round the fo'castle door, like a crowd of dogs watching two other dogs fighting. Jack was there on his bunk and couldn't take his eyes off the horrible scene. One of them got his man up against the bulkhead, pinning him there by the throat with his left hand, while his right went up to pluck the little brass fire extinguisher from the rack over his head. Jack could see the muscles of his back ripple as he brought the deadly weapon down—see the glazed horror in the other man's eyes as he tried to dodge. Then down came the extinguisher, hitting him right between the eyes. He slipped down to the deck as a red, gluey mask covered his face. The winner threw the fire extinguisher on to Jack's bunk—there was a little tuft of greying hair stuck to it by skin and flesh. Then he turned to go out. But the mate confronted him—with a revolver. "Stand still!" was the order—clash, as a set of handcuffs were thrown on to the table. "Shackle that man!" Two men ran across to get him. But he dived at the mate, knocked him flying, scattered the men around the door, and vanished along the deck. He was down the gangway and away into the night before the others had collected their scattered wits. He was never caught—never even seen again. His opponent, wailing feebly for him, was carried ashore.

Next day the ship sailed again. After a week at sea the order came through to go to Rotterdam. All hands brightened up, and the gloom was dispelled a little when the men realised that they were homeward bound. Across the line, back through the Red Sea, through Suez and into the Mediterranean. They steamed past Malta and Gibraltar, and Jack felt as though he was coming to the top of his own street when they reached the Bay of Biscay— the Channel—and then Rotterdam. It was cold. Bitterly, horribly, freezingly cold. The sort of cold that, after the heat of the Persian Gulf, paralyses a man and drives him, blue and shaking, to cower over the galley fire. Jack felt it even worse than the others, for he had no warm clothes. They tied up at Vlaardingen, and he was allowed ten guilders to take ashore. Being still very young and having still the remaining gloss of a decent upbringing, he went to the pictures, and later he went out and had quite a nice supper, then walked back to the ship.

During the trip Jack had not been with any women. Chiefly because he was afraid. Their eyes, the eyes of the prostitute all the world over gave him the cold shivers, the smell of their bodies sickened him. And there was that crawling horror of which he had always been warned—a "dose". Drink never even occurred to him.

They left Rotterdam and beat down the Channel to Falmouth where he was paid off and received his first discharge book. It was stamped and signed; it held his description—very good for conduct—very good for work—and he was very proud of it. He thought "I'll go home—I'll throw my book and pay-off on the table, and I'll say, 'I wanted to go to sea and I went. I'm a success.' And the family will fall down and worship." That's what he thought.

He got his railway warrant and went home. Bought a huge and most exciting meal on the train, and arrived at about seven-fifteen at night. His father had just come home from work when Jack walked in with a creditable imitation of a sailor's roll. He was not well received.

It was not until many years later, when recalling the scene of his first homecoming that he realised the pain and the disappointment that he had caused his parents. He was young, had a certain superficial learning and, when necessary, a charming manner. They had great hopes for him. But he had given them heartaches and trouble by his stupidity and obstinacy. It was bad enough for him to have left them in such a manner without even writing. Bad enough that he had come back as a deck-boy—his nice clothes ruined, and his hands coarse and dirty. But he had begun to swear—a thing never allowed, and scarcely heard of in the house. They warned him, they pleaded with him. But youth is very cruel—youth doesn't give a tinker's cuss for age or experience and, because he met with a certain criticism, Jack felt hurt. If he had attempted to win his father over, his father undoubtedly would have arranged an apprentice-ship for him with some recognised company.

But Jack went back to Falmouth and signed on to another tanker. Quite the old "sea dog" and with a working idea of how to behave himself.

The bosun and chief officer were pretty good fellows, and, as he had had enough of kicks and unpleasantness to last him a long time, Jack did behave himself.

They went out again to Abadan. He fitted into the life of the ship and found out exactly the meaning of life at sea. For him, anyway. There was always enough food, there was always work to do; and if that work was done quietly and well then no one ever bothered him.

Bosun and chippy shared a room in the fo'castle; and he was allowed to poke his head in at the door and listen to the talk. Talk always of ships. Tankers, freighters, Canadian lake boats, whale boats; all the countless tales you could read.

He heard of life on board a ship when a man had to climb the ratlines and chip the ice off the shackles to free them. Of men sweating and toiling in the 'tween decks of whale factories—sliding about in the thick grease as she rolled her scuppers under and men were crushed against the ship's side. Of months laying in the South Atlantic, under a cloudless sky, on a cable ship—groping blindly along the bed of the ocean for the lost end. Months and months of every extreme of weather and discomfort; without music, without literature, without women. Only work and monotony. And of going ashore, starved of all things men want; where they work out their strength and their loneliness on the unresisting bodies of paid women on some foreign shore.

It was about this time that Jack started to drink. An ordinary seaman had been put ashore at Abadan with heatstroke, and Jack was promoted. They were allowed a tot of rum each Saturday, and he liked the rum; or rather he liked the picture of himself in the bosun's room pouring out a tot—or having it poured out for him—and drinking with the men. He had grown a good three inches; he had put on a lot of weight; he had learnt to fight, and he could hold his own.

They got to Aden and he went ashore with the boys for the first time. He had beer, which he liked, because he was thirsty, and he had twenty rupees—which is a lot of money. Into the bar came a woman. She was about thirty-five, black hair, black eyes. A beautiful sunburn brown. He had never seen a Persian woman before and he thought her wonderful; as wonderful as a virgin of seventeen can think of a woman of thirty-five. He could feel a rising tide of excitement. Others had done the same, so why not he? Why should not he, the sailor, take his woman? Thus spoke seventeen years.

It was so very easy to arrange and so quickly over. The others paid five rupees, he paid fifteen. He was robbed of the remainder, and at 2 a.m. was rowed back to the ship by a silent and contemptuous Arab to whom he gave his last eight annas. When he went into the fo'castle and looked in the mirror he got a shock. He looked greasy, drunk, and lecherous. He swore passionately to himself that it was foul and beastly and that he would never do it again; and full of these good resolutions, he turned in. The next night he borrowed five rupees from the bosun, went ashore, and had her again.

When they were a week out he got over all the last lingering repentance and started to boast. Because he had a trick of description and a sense of humour this went down well, and he gained a sort of popularity.

Back in Falmouth he re-signed with the ship as ordinary seaman, learned to drink properly, and now considered himself an old stager. He bought oilskins, sea-boots and a knife. Whilst there he met a girl. A rather sweet little telephone operator who was on holiday. It is extremely improbable that she believed his statement that he was chief officer but never wore uniform ashore. Anyhow, she did give him a little taste of what it was like to know a girl who wasn't always thinking of her last embrace—or how much money she'd be getting for this one. And so back to sea.

There is a particularly bad job which has to be done on a tanker for which all hands get an extra five pounds. It is known as "cleaning tanks." All the spirit or oil left in the tank when a cargo has been discharged has to be taken out; the sides cleaned and scraped. The tank top is then sealed up and steam pressure put in to shift the sludge, which seeps into the bottom of the tanks or at the corners. Now if a man happens to touch these heaps it disturbs the gas—the gas comes out—and out goes the sailor. Flat out. He is then hauled up on the deck, is revived, and immediately goes into laughing hysterics. He is taken out of that with a tot of rum and is sent back down the tank with a splitting headache. Sometimes there are seven tanks to clean.

There was an able seaman on board this trip. He was large and friendly, and his success with women was notorious. Jack didn't like him. They were both in the deep tank, crawling up and down the sides and arguing like hell, when Jack got a whiff of gas and passed out. It was dark and cold in the tank—the fumes were overpowering. His wooden clogs hurt. A tiny little square of light came through the tank top, seemingly miles above them. They scrambled about in the filth and the stink, and they quarrelled. Jack passed out. He was brought up to the deck and revived, then sent below again. He found his scraper had gone and of course he thought that his enemy had taken it. They argued, blows were exchanged, and both went up on deck to fight it out. It was a terrific fight. Jack's nose was broken, and streamed with blood that ran down his chest. The man took one terrific jolt in the throat and went back. Slipped, and teetered against the rail of the tank top—almost went over for a forty-foot drop—caught his balance—and slid back again down on to the deck. Along came the mate and up to the bridge went Jack. The whole stupid story came out and he was logged one pound. How he lorded it over the rest of the fo'castle.

Everything has to be paid for so don't run up too big a bill for yourself. That's a very old saying and a very true one. Jack's credit was stretched to the limit. He was then about nineteen—was getting sailor's pay—and he felt very confident. Nothing had ever happened to upset his opinion of himself. With a moustache he imagined himself to have the beginnings of good looks; with his strength, his pretence of a better education, and plenty of cash he was cock of his own little dunghill. He knew nothing of the years of toil behind some of his shipmates. He knew nothing of the wives and mothers who have to be left allotments. He didn't know, and had never bothered to see, how the black gang toiled and slaved in the bowels of the ship. He knew nothing. He had it all to learn.

Two trips later he started on the second page of his discharge book. He was paid off in his home port and went back to his parents. They were looking so old and tired that he decided he would stay at home for a spell—live on what he had saved. By then he was twenty.

With his beautiful belief in himself he took on all sorts of jobs, selling and canvassing.

Then he met a girl. He met her one warm summer evening. They talked. She was blonde, beautiful and twenty-four—so sweetly spoken that he fell in love with her; told her he was twenty-six—he looked it, and he could talk like it. All his latent inferiority complex came to the surface when he was confronted by her sweetness, good manners, and obvious sincerity. She alone taught him all he knew of clothes, politeness, and good behaviour. It was sweet to be out with her—sweet to be ashore. He had visions of settling down, with a nice home, and a beautiful wife.

So, for her sake because he loved her, his father's because he expected it, and his mother's because she wanted to be proud of him, he decided to stay ashore and get a job. It was very simple—all he had to do was to find the job. There came the difficulty. He had no trade and no experience. No knowledge. Only a great belief in himself, founded on ignorance and pride. He turned to each and every job he could think of—finally landed one. Trying to sell vacuum cleaners. Never in his life had he met quite so many plain damned stupid people. It was hell. Dick, his old school mate, was away—either at sea or on a tramp. Tom used to come home from trips, and by his very silence pleaded with Jack to go back to sea. Joe was working night and day on his father's fishing boat and was rarely seen. Harry, very much the ship's officer, was third mate on a tanker; and he never troubled to conceal his distaste for the job Jack had found. But the girl stuck to him bravely and defended him against all-comers. She had a touching and infinite faith in him—she tried so hard to sell him the idea that he would make a success of his life. But it was no good. He was on a commission basis and didn't even get his expenses. He used blandishments on housewives that would have sold ice cream to an Eskimo. But no good. They either couldn't, or wouldn't afford his machine. He saw the insides of some of the queerest houses. Full of the joy of an imminent sale he cleaned carpets and furniture from top to bottom; dragged layers of dirt from coat sleeves; shampooed hair and was then told "no thank you." The house had been spring cleaned and the housewife was happy. But it nearly broke Jack's heart. He developed a strong starboard list, carrying the goddamn thing about; and clergyman's throat was no joke for him—he had it—often.

The result was a foregone conclusion. Taking his girl out, living at a rate that vastly exceeded his income, something had to happen. And it did. Lacking education or training, cursed with the complete inability to see things in their proper perspective, Jack stole. It was very simply done—delightfully easy. He broke into a house.

It was on a bright summer's day, but Jack was bored and miserable. He couldn't get an answer at the front door so he went round to the back. The back door was locked, but a window was open. He felt an irresistible desire to get inside the house and have a look round. After ten minutes of careful looking around—ten minutes packed with excitement—he found fifteen pounds. And he took it.

The police were on his track almost immediately. He was arrested and taken to the local prison; a horrible place with long, dark, echoing halls interlaced with steel galleries; gloom and depression—and the filthy, loathsome smell of stopped up lavatories; the complete negation of all that is clean and beautiful in life.

He was arrested while over in Liverpool, and his parents discovered the news two days later. His mother came to see him but he refused to see her. He was dragged out. And in a bare little room, watched over by warders, whilst a furtive and rather filthy young man spoke in undertones to a woman, Jack sat and looked at his mother. She had brought him some cake, and she had been crying. They spoke for about twenty minutes, and Jack went back to his cell to sit and stare, to watch the light fading from the window, to think of the peace and warmth of his home, and the unutterable degradation that had come upon him.

He was sent up for trial. The judge looked at him—an awe-inspiring figure. "We have decided that the only thing we can do for you, the only way in which you will be able to straighten out your life, is to send you to a Borstal Institution for three years."

A week later, handcuffed, he was taken down to London, and to Wormwood Scrubs where, for three months, he was given the minimum of food and made to work.

From there he was sent to Nottingham—where he saw all there is to see of moral degradation and perversion.

Boys from the uttermost slums—the dregs of the cities of England—worked and lived there, side by side.

Because at heart he was not a bad boy, Jack got on pretty well; particularly at physical training. There was a large instructor, ex-army heavyweight, who took an interest in him; coached him in the arts of boxing and gymnastics, and tried very hard to convince him that he still had a future.

Jack didn't try any fighting amongst the boys; one unmerciful thrashing soon cured that.

He found the tremendous solace of books—and occasionally music.

The dreadful times were in the summer, when the boys would be locked in their rooms in broad daylight, at eight o'clock in the evening; to lie back in bed and watch the evening sky dotted with skylarks; to hear the rumble of the traffic; and to know that the door was locked.

Looking out one evening he saw a man and a girl sitting down on a grassy bank. The man had his arm around the girl and he was kissing her. These things were denied to Jack. Love and companionship; and the feeling that a twenty-year-old boy has of the world opening out like a beautiful flower when there are things to be done, places to go, and plans to be made.

It wasn't so bad in the winter, working outside all day in the hard, ice-bound fields; to come back at five o'clock tired and weary, wash in cold water, and sit down to a tea of bread and butter.

And once a week a spoonful of jam. And once a fortnight a little cake.

One evening when all was locked and barred and the house had settled down to uneasy slumber, there came a screaming, choking gurgle from the cell below. The hurrying rustle of feet, the slam of a steel door and the frantic blowing of whistles.

Next morning the horror-struck tale was told; of how the night watchman had rushed into a cell and found a limp figure hanging by its belt from the bars of its cage. ...

And one afternoon two cowering, wretched figures were found in one of the lavatories. Two ignorant little perverts were taken out and thrashed.

He had to go—he had to get out of the place.

On the horizon was a large green field and at the top of it, in the centre, a little clump of trees. He'd make for there. He'd run, and run, and run. … Maybe he would be caught—Who cares? Maybe sent back to Wormwood Scrubs—What matter? Anything to get away.

But he never had the courage to do it. He stayed on.

They taught him how to navvy; they taught him how to say Sir; they taught him blind, implicit obedience. And nothing else.

Many and many a time he'd sit in his lonely cell and think of the times he was at sea. The cool, fresh morning air; the wind singing through the mast. The coffee drunk at midnight, thick and black as treacle, warm and comforting. Going ashore on a sunny morning—having a drink—meeting people. Being able to hold up one's head and say, "I'm doing my job."

Conrad and Masefield helped, but he could never escape the awful little room, the plank bed and the mattress, the folded blankets. The memories.

Hope died, faith died. Nothing left but an automaton—wandering through life, down the gloomy corridors of time, fulfilling its allotted task—a prisoner.

One morning, after two years and three months, they released him. Dressed in a neat grey suit, he was taken down to the station and put on the train. He had eight and threepence halfpenny in his pocket and his ticket home. He had a faintly bewildered feeling that somewhere in that dreadful building he had left something—something that is called a soul.

He went home. He went home and was welcomed, was fed and was forgiven.

He saw his girl once. Walking down the street, striding along, whistling happily at the thought of being home, he came round the corner and almost ran into her. Jack's heart gave one sickening leap, he was bereft of words. She saw him, gave him one tragic look, and passed him by.

He met Tom again. Tom, very sunburned and very quiet. They went into a pub for a drink and Tom learned the whole story. He stood there, with his hands in his overcoat pockets, and let Jack talk himself out. Then he said, "Elder & Fyffes are signing a ship on Saturday. Coming along?" Jack joined the ship on Saturday.

It was good to be back at sea: yet it was hell. He had the feeling that he had been cheated. Why hadn't he been able to make a go of it on shore? Slaving about in the wind and cold, whilst officers stalked the bridge and ordered him about. Strange—there he was on a good ship, good feeding, easy work, and officers who were gentlemen—and he thought like that.

He wasn't popular on board. He was late on watch, he put on airs and he fought. It seemed a good thing to him to take to the rule of the fist. And, as he had no real opponents on board, it was easy. He was as strong as a horse and very fit—just spoiling for a fight; and just about ready, had he but known it, for the lesson of his life.

He arrived at Kingston, Jamaica, with the dead certainty of a black discharge. So he went ashore and got drunk—on rum—at threepence a tot and two shillings a bottle. He was adrift for three days and went back aboard in a bad state.

The ship headed down south to Santa Marta, where he repeated his performance of Kingston, this time on tequila—a sort of white poison that only the lowest Mexicans and bad whites ever drink. Three hours before the ship was due to sail he was dragged from a café in a state that defies description.

He was unconscious when they carried him aboard and didn't recover properly for days. He had done no washing the whole time—and very little work. The black discharge at the end of the voyage was as inevitable as the sun setting in the west.

They reached Montego Bay. Lovely pellucid green waters, waving trees, softly spoken black people. He went ashore and he stayed ashore. From the top of the hill he watched his ship pull out. He could hear the rattle of the winch as the hook came up, see the boys fore and aft as they worked—see the churning water under her stern as she drifted away from the stage. He stood there a deserter, and he liked it.

It was so easy to live at Montego Bay. A lot of society people used to stay there at the one big hotel. There was a little mixed race girl who took him to the bosom of her family, and all was well. With about four pounds in his possession he lived well. Life was one beautiful round of swimming, fishing, and selling hard luck stories to credulous people who had nothing better to do than to listen to them. Long, dreamy days and nights, and again he was cock of the walk. He stayed there for two—nearly three months.

Then one day a ship pulled in, and he got homesick. The ship, seen from the top of the hill, seemed indescribably filthy. A blot on that beautiful bay. But he went on board. He could have got home as a Distressed British Seaman at a shilling a month, but as he had run out of money, and there was none waiting for him at home, he wanted to get a job.

The skipper was small, dapper, and very sure of himself. Yes, she was going home. He could have a job as a trimmer. Had he a discharge book? No? Sign here. He did. And that night the ship sailed.

The crew was mixed. The rough gang consisted of two Estonians, one Sunderland man, three black men, an American-Irishman and two Swedes. The cook was a Romanian.

Jack was put on the twelve to four watch, and the food he got from the galley stank. The fo'castle was an evil-smelling, festering hole, with a rusty bogey in the centre. His bed was a donkey's breakfast with one blanket that had a large brown, stiff patch of congealed blood—or something else—in the middle. The place had the loathsome, horrifying smell of bugs, that permeated the whole ship. There were no cockroaches; the bugs had eaten them as they had died of starvation. But there were rats.

There was no free water—the issue was one-half bucket per day, per man—perhaps. The lavatory was a cubicle, minus a door, in the steering flats. In it was a large cast-iron drain with a hole in the top, one end leading over the side and the other flushed from the deck supply by a length of old hosepipe. When there was no water on deck you couldn't flush it. When there was water the outlet was stopped up. The smell was terrific; and it was the condiment to every meal Jack had on board. The flies were murderous.

With the Estonians and the Yank, who was a greaser, Jack went down the long endless ladder, past the quivering engines—grease and dirt deep around him—into the stokehold. The heat was terrifying. He went along into the bunkers, and there was a large, battered shovel and a huge wheelbarrow. He knew how they felt in the days of the Spanish Inquisition when the torturer came up with the rack. Softened with easy living—wringing wet with sweat—he kept murmuring to himself, "Go on—get stuck into it—you'll be home in two weeks." His hands blistered within an hour, and he was choked with coal dust. The two squareheads stolidly fired, pitched, sliced and cleaned. He felt as though his back was breaking. His shoulders were being torn from their sockets. Pieces of coal got into his shoes. The wobbly wheel of the barrow would lurch and the load would shift. The watch lasted an eternity. He was relieved at eight bells and went up with the Yank. "How long will it take to get to England?" he asked, through the layers of coal dust in his gullet. The Yank looked at him long and hard, and said, "She's not going East. She's going to San Pedro via the Canal." Jack was so dead beat that the enormity of this statement did not penetrate at the time.

He went aft, stumbling like a drunken man; heading for the haven of a sailor's rest—his bunk. But he had to have a wash, and there was no water. The pump was locked. Through red and half-blind eyes he peered around for a bucket that might have a drop of filthy water in it; he might just as well have looked for a bottle of Napoleon brandy in his lice-ridden pallet. In the end he tied a length of rope to an old leaky bucket—lowered it over the side, hauled it up—and tried to swill the coal dust off with salt water. It was about as easy as you'd expect it to be. The black coal dust refused to leave the safe sanctuary of his hair. The rising pimples of his old friend, prickly heat, rose under his arms. Ten minutes of futile splashing about and he gave the job up. His hands had started to bleed and he just couldn't take it. He crawled to his bunk. Out of sheer surprise the bugs made room for him.

What a ship—she was a sailor's Gethsemane. And Jack used to like to think of the day when she'd be coming back from some trip and her drunken swine of a skipper would try to take her a short cut across Ireland.

Second day at sea he took stock of his surroundings and found she was a thirty-five-year-old tramp—eight thousand tons. No refrigerator, one small ice box—not in use—no ventilation or fans, no linen, no soap. And the skipper owned seventy-five per cent of her. Two men had died of the original crew—some had deserted. The skipper, the mate, the two senior engineers and the Sunderland man—Jordy—were the only original members of the crew. And she was out on tramp indefinitely. Jack got a little soft soap from the cook, tried to clean himself, and partly succeeded. Tried to clean his bunk, and failed. He gave up the blanket as entirely gratuitous torture, and waited for the seven bell dinner. Salt beef with maggots, and biscuits with weevels. For the rest of his life he had to remember not to tap his bread on the table before eating it. On that ship it became automatic.

It began to penetrate into his head that he had landed in a tough spot but he hoped he could handle it. He was wrong.

The Third engineer didn't like the two squareheads, and the steam was falling. Jack took a spell and watched him, as he came into the stokehold—arguing in his high-pitched, South Wales voice. The Estonians just looked at him. The Third gave out an insult, an original insult, an insult that reached an all-time high in filth. He was going through the door when a lump of coal, weighing about seven pounds, caught him in the small of the back.

When a man is hit like that he doesn't bleed—a thin black line of blood, and grease, and sweat, appears on his back as he lies there and doesn't move. It forms a thicker line—trickles down his back, round his kidneys and on to the stokehold plates. There is a faint, filthy smell of burning hair: the plates are hot.

The Estonian walked over to him, rolled him over, looked objectively at him and kicked him dispassionately right in the pelvis. The Third almost sat up, his eyes black with pain. Another kick, same place, and he fell forward with his head between his knees. The Estonian grabbed him by the hair and dragged him into the engine room. The clang of the bell was heard as he rang the ship to stop; then he came back. Down came the Chief—the steam was almost non-existent—the Third was taken up—and the ship was put under way again. No one said anything to the squarehead. It was that sort of ship. The Chief took the four to eight watch, the

Second took the twelve to four and the Fourth took the eight to twelve. That night the Third engineer died and was buried without the benefit of clergy.

Jack carried on—retreating deeper into himself. Speaking to no one, eating what food he could. He gave up trying to be clean and lived not like an animal but like some loathsome degenerate.

Daily the heat increased. His shoes split and tore, and his hands became hard with great thick ridges of leathery callous across the palms.

One day the Yankee accused him of stealing a sweat-rag. He hadn't, told him so and called him a liar. They were standing on the stokehold plates, the air was thick with tiny particles of dust and the revolting smell of wet ashes. Both of them were filthy and unshaven; wracked with prickly heat and poisoned with bad food. The consciousness of his decline had clouded Jack's brain for some time—he felt a rising tide of anger choke him; he was trembling with rage and fear. The Yank was a tough customer. He made one swipe at Jack, catching him a clout over the head that seemed to jar every tooth loose. He went down and the Yank got on top of him.

It's a strange thing when a man is fighting, thoughts of the past always run through his head. Jack thought of the time when he had fought Mr. George Smith on the grass outside St. James's Church. He remembered a trick and, arching his knees, gave the Yank a terrific push, sending him flying over his head. Jack was up and round like a flash, leapt on the man, and was going to brain him with his own spanner when he saw his eyes. They were frantic with an animal terror; he was almost livid. Jack couldn't hit him. He dragged him to his feet, spun him round and told him just what he would do if he worried him again. Then with one strong push he sent the Yankee flying. Jack turned, and was heading for the ladder when the spanner whistled past his head. If he had stopped it his few remaining brains would have traced a simple and very bloody pattern all over the gauge glass. Throughout all this the two squareheads and the engineer had said nothing. Jack went back to his bunkers, his barrow, and his thoughts.

They arrived at San Pedro, and Jack went ashore with Jordy. They had a ten-buck note each and they went into the first bar they came across. Jack saw himself in the long, flyblown mirror behind the bar. He remembered the dapper fellow of almost four years ago, with his polished shoes and beautifully pressed suit; his clean linen and his boundless optimism. He remembered his girl and summer afternoons when they swam; sweet moments as they stepped out of the car. St. James's Church, when five little boys sang the Te Deum and Adeste Fideles. Long walks along the promenade saying good morning to friends. The man in the mirror behind the bar gazed imploringly at him. He was tall and thin—carefully scratching himself. He had a semi-beard, through which could be seen a sallow, fish-belly complexion. A dirty flannel shirt—wide open—covered him. Half-way down his chest was a thick ridge of dirt and grease, with runnels of sweat tracing white lines down it. Jack looked down and could see his own dungaree trousers at the mirror head—dark with patches of sweat. They could—and frequently did—stand up by themselves. An indescribable odour of stale uncleanliness drifted up. The man in the mirror continued to look at him until a push from the bartender made him turn round. "Drink up," said the bartender. "Get it down and beat it. We don't encourage no bums or wild bastards here." The man in the mirror looked hopelessly at Jack, drank his measure of rum and went out. Jordy had said nothing.

They trudged along the sidewalk, found at length a bar lower than Jack had ever seen before, and they went in. Two immaculate Yankee sailors were there, but at the sight of Jack and Jordy they went out. The girls wouldn't even look at them. They sat and drank. At length a woman came in and sat down; she was very fat, very smelly, and rather drunk. Jack looked up and felt such a wave of nausea—at himself and her—that he couldn't even speak. She got up and wobbled over—sweet with the aroma of generations of garlic and sloth. She popped the question to Jordy and one dollar was arranged as a fee. He followed her heaving rump upstairs. Jack ordered another drink. Ten minutes later Jordy came down, and said, "Not bad, chum—best we can expect." We can expect— he was right. How long they sat drinking Jack didn't know. Then he heard Jordy's voice, quiet and soft in its accent and sweet with the pathos of remembered joys: "That was before your time, sonny, when music halls were all the go. She used to be a maid at one of the big gentlemen's houses. I done a few trips on the Pacific Steam Navigation Company, then I came ashore and I met her. We used to go out every Saturday night to the old Rotunda. I was in good shape in these days. Well, she said she'd marry me and we had it all fixed. I got a job on a coal cart." Then his voice changed: "She took ill—stoppage of the bowels, they called it. She was dead in a week. Funny—nothing seemed to go right after that—and I went back to sea. I started soaking pretty heavy and I lost all my good companies. Now I'm on this job—been on her three years. I don't know why I stay; she's such a lousy, bloody ship. But I'm just not going to let it beat me like everything else has. I'll drive her till she kills me like she's killed others." His voice trailed away, and Jack looked at him—with his ragged white moustache, grey hair, and the look of dreadful resignation that came over his face as the glow of his memories left him. Was he an old forty or a young sixty? Wonder what he used to look like, thought Jack. Did this derelict wear stand-up collar and peg-topped trousers, like he used to see. Suppose he felt just like I used to with my girl, he thought. Then a voice inside him murmured, "How very sweet. He started like you, and you'll finish like him." Jordy looked up at him—very suddenly—and said, "Come on, Jack, let's leave the booze alone and do some shopping. Let's get some soap and some dungarees." They went out—but they never bought any gear. They stopped at the next bar and stayed there. The bartender stole their remaining dollars when they passed out. On board, when they had recovered, they found that the two Estonians had jumped ship and two more black men had signed on. So Jordy and Jack took what was left of the squareheads' gear.

Like Cain, Jack wandered the face of the earth; and like Cain he was branded. His nose was broken and he'd lost his side teeth. One dreadful night he had his eyebrows split wide open and his jaw broken. Without rest or respite he wandered outcast—lecherous—and riddled with vermin.

In Melbourne the skipper refused him money, so he went ashore and bummed drinks. He got two—like bones slung to a dog. Then to the Seaman's Mission, very clean and neat. He went to the padre and asked for money. The padre refused, but he offered Jack a bath. It was strange and comforting to lie back in that bath and, after two changes of water, he began to feel clean. He noticed that his job was giving him a perfect condition as far as strength was concerned—but he looked almost with terror at the heap of rags he would have to put on. The padre had thought of this, and had a change of clean clothes ready for him. Feeling fresh, clean and reborn, he stood in front of the mirror and combed his hair. At peace with the world he went down to the hall and met the padre, who gave him a meal and one pound. Then he went out—had a haircut and shave—walked right past all the bars and returned to the Mission. He had tea with the padre, who never once talked religion to him. He talked of world affairs and cooking—and books. He gave Jack a small Bible, told him to read it when he had time, and said good-bye with these words: "Don't jump your ship, she's what you need to straighten you out. Keep on her, work, and try to recapture your love and understanding of beauty. Don't let it get you down."

Jack tried very hard after he left Melbourne. And the height of his success was only equalled by the depth of his failure.

In Brisbane he was well behaved. Bought soap, wrote home, and mixed with a very good crowd of Americans from one of the Export Lines. He felt as though he were rising above the filth of the ship, and he got a queer pleasure from describing how bad she was. He enjoyed Brisbane. From there they went to Calcutta.

Down at the docks, in the heat and discomfort of life on board, he lost all he had ever gained. A few drinks and he felt the need for excitement rise up in him; he went with two of the black men on a tour of the "houses." Then back through the silent main streets, lined with beggars sleeping in the gutter and on the pavements. Being very drunk he started a row—and was mixed up in a multitude of screaming, gesticulating coolies. One of the black men went down in the mob. And as Jack—the tough guy—ran away, he could hear his frightful screams.

After that he saw no use in even trying to keep his head above water. He was driven by his own lust and self-torture. By some sort of miracle he had escaped venereal disease.

At length they reached Cape Town and found, after nearly eighteen months, that they really were going home. Maybe it was the thought of home, maybe the life he had been leading—but one day Jack came up from the bunkers, bullied the cook, got a bucket of hot water and had a bath. He put on the one and only clean singlet he had ever worn on the voyage, and sat on the fo'castle head. He found the little Bible that the Melbourne padre had given him and he started to read it. And he found the story of how our Lord had said: "Suffer little children to come unto Me, for of such is the Kingdom of Heaven."

The Kingdom of Heaven was what he had dreamed of with a girl back home. They used to sit on the promenade and talk of what they would have—and do. Of a sweet little house—with her cooking for him. She would be so spotless and neat—and he would bring his friends home, and they would admire her so much. Then one day she would tell him—and they would await the arrival of their son. He would be their Kingdom of Heaven.

He sat on the fo'castle and dreamed. The sun went down in a blaze of glory and the sea was quiet and still; the evening sky darkened. Lying on his back he saw the moon come out and up with her attendant star. One by one the stars twinkled out, and the lonely albatross that had followed them all day hid himself in the boundless wastes of his ocean home. With the gentle, lullaby rhythm of the sea, the stars seemed to swing backwards and forwards—almost touching the stark outlines of the foremast. His old friends the porpoises came out and did their set of lancers in front of the bows. He could hear the rustle and swish of their bodies as they surfaced. And the gentle plop as they submerged. The sea, the sky, the moon and the stars—in unison—told him of the glorious heritage of beauty that belongs to the sailor. They would forgive him all, so long as he was worthy of them and could feel their beauty. In procession he saw those men of the sea whose names have been handed down to us. Erik the Red in his Viking ship—Columbus, who sailed out into the unknown—Magellan, who braved the Horn with the knowledge that men with courage would win—Drake—and Bully Forbes, who drove the *Lightning* in a gale across the Western Ocean, to do the passage in eleven days. And he saw the sailors of 1914–1918. Wrecked, sunk, torpedoed, starved and driven mad. But who had sailed—who had taken ships out and brought ships back.

For the first time in his life he realised the traitor he had been to himself. And, for the first time in his life, he prayed.

That night he went below and the shovel was nothing—the barrow a mere handful. He even found it in his heart to like the ship. She had tried him and beaten him—all that was undisciplined in him she had brought out—but he had triumphed. They beat across the Bay of Biscay and he sang at his work. In turn he bribed and robbed the steward for soap and cleaned what he had of gear. At last, in Cardiff, they paid off and he was free. They had been away nearly two years.

He bought a new rig-out and then went back to the docks to see the ship there, silent and aloof. In dock her grotesque appearance was even more noticeable. There she lay—the Sailor's Gethsemane.

Jack went home, saw his mother and father again and picked up his old friendships. He met Tom again. They used to meet daily in Liverpool to have a drink. They would arrange to meet at Jack's pub at six-thirty. Jack would be there dead on time, then the door would swing open and in would come Tom—hat on the back of his head, pipe in his mouth, hands thrust deep in his overcoat pockets, and Western Ocean written all over him. He would walk up, nod to the barmaid and say, "Pint, miss." He never said an unnecessary word and he had a fund of common sense larger than any man Jack had met—or so it seemed to him. They met one day and Tom said: "Do you know old Bill who used to be a bosun? Well, he's ashore and sort of retired. Met him last night. Told him I'd get him some Faithful Lover plug tobacco. I've got it and I'll take it up to him to-night." "I've got plenty at home," said Jack, "you can give him some from me." Tom said: "Come up and give it to him yourself."

So the two boys went up to old Bill's house. The tram journey was long, and afterwards they walked down a little avenue, knocked on a door, and a young lady answered.

"Yes, Dad's at home. Won't you come in?" She was a pretty, girl, with a very grave face. She seemed to take things quite seriously as mistress of the house. Jack liked her at sight and, almost at once, he knew he was going to take her out. Tom said nothing. They saw old Bill and he introduced the young lady as his only daughter,

Betty. They stayed there the whole evening, Tom and old Bill deep in conversation. Bill had served his time in sail, which was Tom's hobby. Jack, the opportunist, found time to ask Betty to come out. She agreed, but looked at him as though she wondered why he would ever want to take out a girl like her.

They met two days later. Went to the Empire, the Adelphi—all the places Jack fondly considered the best. He just loved those great, flashy dumps. He was in his element, showing off his knowledge of menus, and other things. The waiters had many a good laugh at his expense.

But one evening he met her when he was very drunk. And she told him quietly and effectively that she didn't want to see him again.

Three weeks later Tom and Betty were engaged.

And Jack went back to the bottle.

He went back to the bottle because he could think of nothing better to do—and because his pride had received another swift kick in its pants. He was still completely on the wrong track, still hadn't benefited from the lesson he had received before—the lesson that a man's integrity is all that matters. He didn't realise—or rather he did but he took no notice—that to try to rise above his present station in life without work and straight thinking would always be attended by ultimate failure. His perfectly good discharge book was now no good to him. Jumping ship at Montego Bay had effectively seen to that. A discharge as a trimmer was of no use, so he would have to start afresh.

He found himself in Falmouth, looking for a job. He arrived at eleven o'clock in the morning—and he started to drink. He continued all that day and all the next day, with very little food: looking back over his life—grieving over lost opportunities—and, of course, thinking himself very badly treated.

On the same evening he met some of the boys and at ten o'clock went to a dance. He was bursting for some sort of disturbance.

And he got it. He was as drunk as ever he had been in his life. In the dance hall were some American sailors from a freighter in the harbour. One asked him his ship, and was answered, "British tanker." The American laughed; "So you're a limey bastard off a bum tanker, eh?" Jack turned and let him have it right in the face. This started a "free-for-all." Jack was thrown out. He went back, and got into the fight again—bursting to get at the American. He got the American. Also a couple of innocent bystanders. He was thrown out on his neck again and a policeman picked him up. Jack turned and belted him, doing considerable damage to his upper set. Then, still drunk, he was down the road like a shot. He saw a car, and without pause or hesitation he got into it and was away like a bat out of hell. What a ride! He screamed round Falmouth, trying to find the Sailor's Home. Right round Castle Drive and headed for the wilds—still drunk. The road forked left-hand up hill, right-hand down hill. He took the left at about forty and saw a white railing in front. Stood on everything and pulled the wheel over. The car just teetered on the edge of the bank, toppled over and lay on her side. The engine gave one choking sob and died. Jack crawled out through the roof. He finished the remainder of the bottle of whisky in his pocket—he had never even taken his coat off at the dance—then he made his way to the Sailor's Home, knocking up all sorts of people on the way, to get directions—leaving a trail of indignant householders from the wrecked car to his bed.

The next morning he was considerably scared and thought of making tracks for the long grass. But the constabulary had not been asleep, he had been recognised as the man who had been so conclusively drunk, and was roped in that morning. For three days he was held in durance vile and was sent up before the magistrate.

Falmouth was agog at its crime wave. The court was quite crowded, and a representative of the local press worked himself into a lather taking down proceedings in laborious long-hand.

Jack spent most of the time wondering how he could pay the inevitable ten-pound fine: he needn't have worried. The magistrate was very old, and very just. He retired to make a decision, then came back. "Young man," he said, "you have all your youth and strength. It would appear that you have had some little education, which makes matters worse. You have deliberately chosen to get yourself so loathsomely drunk that you are incapable of reasonable thought or action. Whilst in this state, you assault a man in the dance hall. You then attack a policeman in the course of his duties. You remove a man's car; a doctor, who might urgently need it. You then drive away in this appalling condition. If you had injured anyone on this mad escapade, I would have sent you for trial. You would have received at least two years' imprisonment. As it is, by God's mercy, you injured no one, and only the car was wrecked. Under these circumstances I can do nothing but sentence you to two months' hard labour. I hope that you will benefit by it."

Jack stood there rigid with shock. All his bounce had gone. The local pressman looked at him curiously as he was led out and walked up the street to the station. And so into Exeter gaol.

It was all done so quietly. The policeman took him up from Falmouth, they sat in the train together, he was brought tea at Plymouth—and cigarettes. And almost apologetically he was handed over to the prison guard. That night he sat looking vacantly at his shoes, realising that once again he was "inside."

It was a queer place to be in. He sewed mail bags all day. The bottom gallery of cells was called Tanker Alley, because of the sailors who always occupied it. The second gallery was known as the Ritz and was full of strange old derelicts who were on the tramp, and who would go to gaol for much the same reason as a normal man would go to the pictures. But the top gallery and its inmates were an enlightenment in itself. This was the end of the easy-going road. Men doing long terms for embezzlement—men who had robbed with violence—men whose lust for women or excitement had led them to the refinements of degradation. They were all there. These were the wise guys.

Throughout that long two months the old magistrate's words rang continually in Jack's mind. "You have all your youth and strength—you would appear to have had some little education." He couldn't forget it. He had no self-pity. Plainly and objectively he could see how he had landed there; where he had made his mistake; and why he never stood a chance with Betty. He kept quiet, got full remission, was released in due course, and sent back to Falmouth.

Somewhere in the back of his head was the idea that he was now a gaol bird—a convicted criminal. He was going straight in the future, but he expected very little help on the subject of how.

He had to report to the police station and announce his arrival. He was interviewed by the chief constable, given some money to get a meal and was told to come back afterwards. He did, feeling much better. The chief constable sat him down, then he said: "First, here is one pound to tide you over; I'll arrange to get you some more. We've got a room for you at the Sailor's Home—you'll be all right there for your food and bed. The shipping master knows you're back—I have given you a recommendation and you'll get the first ship out, and a good job. Away you go—and keep off the drink."

He was ashore there for six weeks, and enjoyed himself more than he had for years. Swimming, walking over the hills—he got more sunburned than ever he had been, even in the tropics. Finally he got a ship—a tanker—and pushed off again, in a good rig-out presented by the Sailor's Home.

She was a happy ship. The accommodation was really good and the food excellent; and he was really doing some hard, good work. Throughout the whole trip he remained sober and industrious.

It was at Las Palmas that he saw the effects of war and starvation. Jack had led a selfish life: if he had been in danger, it was his own fault—he had sought it: if he had been hungry, he could have avoided it: and if he had been broke, he was young and strong—and could put that right any time. But in Las Palmas he found people who were in fear of death, hunger and penury—and couldn't lift a hand to save themselves. He saw Fascism—the results of it; and it wasn't a pleasant sight.

They reached Las Palmas one lovely spring morning and tied up at the Mole. He had just helped to tie up aft with the second mate and the remainder of the watch, and when everything was finished he stood by the break of the poop and lit a cigarette. There was a large, motley crowd, very dispirited, walking along the Mole. They were all calling for food—trying to attract the attention of the men on board—tapping their mouths or stomachs. Men, women and children. One gets used to the average sailor who comes on board for food, he lives that way. But these people were obviously in earnest. There was one old lady who kept very quiet but, whenever she caught Jack's eye, the naked appeal in her face turned his heart with pity. He turned round and saw Slush, the cook, coming up from the refrigerator. In his hand he held the long strip of gristle and skin that is cut from the back of a sheep and is, presumably, no good for eating. At least it wasn't on that ship, where they fed like fighting cocks. He came up on deck and slung the refuse into the bin, then he disappeared into the galley. Jack was going to give the old lady his breakfast—he wasn't very hungry. More for a joke than anything else—because he knew she was going to be fed—he went to the bin, took the meat out and held it up for her. She almost went crazy, executing a delirious sort of hop in pleasure and anticipation—waving frantically to him. He put the meat under the tap and washed it, then beckoned to her as he walked along the poop, down the ladder and across the after well-deck to the gangway. She walked along the Mole, collecting a gesticulating mob. He handed it to her as a policeman came along. The policeman pushed the old lady on one side and took the meat himself.

Now you will realise that Jack in his life had had his fill of trouble; he had fallen foul of the law on many occasions. He was on a good ship, and he didn't want to spoil his record. But he did what any man would do—he gave the policeman one under the chin that put his tonsils somewhere round by his collar stud. The policeman went out cold. The old lady got the meat.

Jack went and told all hands, and no one on board had breakfast that morning. They held picnic parties on the jetty—and dished out curry and rice, porridge, mutton chops and potatoes.

Soon the damaged policeman appeared at the bottom of the gangway with a squad of the local gendarmerie, demanding that the person of Jack should be handed over to the law. Jack retired to the bilges down in the engine room. The ship was searched— and the crew was most unhelpful. The search party then went to the galley. They threatened, bullied, and cajoled the cook— who treated them with the silent contempt that a six-foot-three Scotsman will always show for anything other than another six-foot-three Scotsman.

That night the boys went ashore. All sailors know Doris's bar at Las Palmas—the first stop outside the dock gate. Everybody liked old Doris; she had run a bar for sailors in Hamburg—she was a Cockney—and she was driven out by the Nazis. She told the boys of conditions on shore, and she told them the reason for the shortage of food. Mr. Franco was getting worried about the Non-Intervention stunt in Spain: so all his troops who were wounded or useless were shipped off to Las Palmas; without pay, hospitals, or barracks. Italians, Germans, Moors, Natives—the whole issue. Bad men—some of them out for any mischief.

And this is how they were fed. The price of every commodity was doubled. You put down two pesetas for a box of matches; one for the box, and one for a little coloured card with "To subsidise the Army" printed in the centre. You put the matches in your pocket, you tore up the card, and the peseta went to the soldiers. This applied to everything—food, drink, clothes, transport, etc. If you had an arrangement with the vendor and didn't pay this tax, a soldier or a spy might be there. You were quadruple fined and the goods were taken off you to become the immediate property of the soldier who found you out. He extorted the fine and he also kept it. It was nice work for the soldiers and they kept their eyes peeled.

They left the bar and went back to the ship—she was sailing that night. Half-way down the Mole they were met by the search party. Old Spanish courtesy was at a discount, and the police got, not what they looked for, but what they asked for. It was very lucky for the boys that the ship sailed that night.

After that trip Jack went home, and was best man at Tom's wedding.

It was a lovely, very beautiful summer—and he spent it on the beach, with the *Silver Foam*—a pleasure launch. Dick was there too—and Tom—and Joe. And Harry, with his younger brother Peter.

The *Silver Foam* was the smartest boat on the beach, and their rivals, of the *Skylark*, were green with envy as she tore up the river at the rate of knots—three knots. They made a gangway, from the back axle of an old Ford, with some planks—and took it in turn to handle the gangway or run the boat. And what a crew it was! Maybe some very old passenger ship would lie in mid-stream, and Dick would implore the whole beach—in a voice that could be heard over a North Sea gale: "All aboard the *Silver Foam*. Come for a trip round the *Queen Mary*. All aboard—all aboard." From further down the beach would come the howl of a jealous rival: "All aboard the *Skylark*. All aboard the *Skylark*. Round the lighthouse." Then Dick's voice would rise to a bellow: "Sign on the *Silver Foam*. Lovely grub—lovely grub." Trippers would stand abashed, but Dick would walk up and grab the leader of the group by the arm: "We're sailing now. *Silver Foam. Silver Foam*," and then in a hoarse whisper: "Lovely grub."

One morning they missed Dick. The beach was crowded—but no sign of the truant. They ate his fish and chips at one o'clock; they drank his tea and wondered where he had gone. There was still no sign of his stalwart figure at two-thirty. The pubs had closed and they noticed a mob coming down the beach. And in the centre of the crowd was Dick—as delightfully drunk as it is possible to be. With thrilling tales of his magnificent craft he had brought down every customer in the pub; and, as he shepherded them on board, he was whispering into the ears of all the pretty mill girls, "Lovely grub, lovely grub."

Jack would always look back on that beautiful summer; the *Silver Foam*, the soft warm air—the bathes—the dances, and walks back home along a moonlit promenade—with a feeling that it marked an epoch in his life.

He hadn't bothered much more with any girls, and he told his friends, "I'd only marry an intelligent woman, and no intelligent woman will ever marry me." Dick had a better line on the subject, and remarked, "He won't marry 'em when he's sober, and they won't look at him when he's drunk." In any case Jack realised that even if he did find a girl he had nothing to offer her. He hoped and waited and dreamed.

That magic summer drew to a close and the boys went their various ways. Jack went back to sea on a British tanker.

September the third, 1939. A hundred miles south-west of Land's End the crew gathered in the cook's room to listen to the news. At 9.30—ship's time—Chamberlain told them they were at war. "It is evil things we are fighting against. Brutality—bad faith."

Leaning against the bunk, Jack thought of many things. Stories of old sailors who had gone through the last war. Shellings, sinkings, torpedoing; and the loathsome, contemptible way in which those sailors had been treated after it. The filthy conditions on board many ships that fly the Red Ensign.

Why should he fight? What did he owe the country? He remembered tales of profiteers during the last war. Would they spring up in this? Would he have to sail out, to risk his life, for food to supply a black market? Why should he fight?

The pattering of feet on deck roused him from his reverie. A destroyer was signalling them to go about and put into Weymouth harbour.

And there, that night, when the ship lay at anchor—reeking with the smell of grey paint, the air foul with the closed port holes—he went up on deck, and realised that there was another side to the question. Evil things! He remembered the story of the fiendish bombing of Guernica—the massacre of the peoples of Spain. He remembered the old lady who had wept for joy when he gave her meat—and the Fascist policeman who had tried to steal it from her. He remembered the cold eyes of the Nazis whom he saw ashore at Hamburg. Then he remembered the Merseyside; his friends; and a soft, warm stretch of country—with the inviolable hills of Wales brooding over all in protection. Suddenly he had a mental picture of England as she could be. It was the fight of the little peoples of the world against oppression and injustice. And what a fight. By God's help, and a belief in the justice of the cause, England would fight and win.

Jack looked round at the men who were his shipmates, and he could see his own thoughts mirrored in their eyes. All hands, from the skipper to the cabin boy, stayed on their ship. They all signed on again when they arrived back at Falmouth.

Jack went ashore—and who should be on the dockyard gate but the policeman whose upper set he had knocked out in that old escapade. As soon as he saw him the policeman came and shook hands—asked him if he was O.K. and then said, "Listen, Jack, when you come back on board, for heaven's sake come back sober. The soldiers are guarding the dock, and if you don't answer the challenge at once they're liable to open fire. Take care now—or you'll get hurt."

This from a policeman whom he had assaulted. Gestapo and Brownshirts, please note!

So Jack didn't get drunk. He had his beer with his shipmates; and later they sailed out in convoy.

His first taste of the convoy system and the zig-zag clock nearly drove him crazy, but it was a lovely sight to see the ships ploughing along. Tankers, freighters, old tramps, passenger liners, armed merchant cruisers and destroyers. It took them a long time—longer than he had ever thought it could—to get to Gibraltar. Then past the Rock and through to Port Said. Down the canal, into the Red Sea, past Aden, Ras al-Hadd, and the Twelve Apostles standing grim and dark against the evening sky. Twelve great, enormous rocks, miles from land, sticking up grim and silent out of the clear water. Taking a blacked-out ship up the Persian Gulf, with the port holes closed at night, was pretty dreadful—and Abadan was even worse than it had been before.

The ship left and headed back for England with about twelve thousand tons of benzine on board. On the way they heard of the tragic end of the *Rawalpindi*—and finally landed at Gibraltar to await convoy. The weather was bitterly cold, and the ship had a breakdown. The convoy sailed out the following week, and four days out they had another breakdown. They were right in the submarine area.

Jack had his first taste of four-on and four-off watches and was getting into his stride. He stood on the poop—scanning the waters with binoculars, looking for submarines. Not afraid of the submarines, not doubting the outcome, but ready to fight to defend the ship whether it were good, bad, or indifferent. This one happened to be indifferent. But they took the ship and her cargo, and landed up in the Clyde. They lay in mid-stream for ten days and then went ashore.

Jack went home, and his street mourned its first dead. Joe was dead. Poor, quiet, stubborn Joe—with his frustrated dreams, his sense, and his one hundred per cent loyalty. He had been Royal Naval Reserve and had gone straight into the *Courageous*. His mother was broken-hearted. Jack met Tom and went back to St. James's Church one Sunday morning—with Harry, young Peter, and Dick—who was minesweeping. And they held their own, very private service of memory and commemoration.

As they came out into the winter sunlight Jack asked Tom what he was doing. "I'm sticking to the sea," said Tom. "I'll take three weeks off and then join the Gun School at Liverpool. Maybe I'll get a smack at those sea-going bastards."

They joined together and learned, in two weeks, how to handle four-inch guns—twelve pounders—and Hotchkiss machine-guns. It was a gruelling fortnight. They passed their course and got their tickets. Jack was now "Merchant Seaman Gunner 9009," under extra pay from the Admiralty—sixpence a day while on Articles.

He took a Harrison boat out to India, and found out that this was a total war. They missed raiders by a hair's breadth. They had scares and alarms—a time when, clad in pyjama trousers only, he shot like a bullet from the quarters to the gun and stood there tense, with his legs rigid in expectation—waiting for the plume of the submarine, or the bubbles like steel helmets on the water, denoting the terrifying path of the torpedo.

But they got the ship to Calcutta with munitions; and back to England with tea. And it was about this time that Jack's hair started to go grey.

He couldn't wait for the ship's four weeks' turn around, so he handed his book to the shipping master and was assigned a ship sailing out at the week-end. Destination unknown.

He went aboard and found rumours that the ship would sail out in about thirty-six hours. He saw no point in going home, so just stayed on board and did gangway watch.

He was leaning over the rail, smoking a pipe and gazing blankly at the stewards as they carried stores aboard. They toiled up the gangway carrying parcels, cases, meat—all the thousand and one things for the needs of a ship at sea. Suddenly something seemed strange to Jack, he looked more closely at the packages and, when his relief came, he said to him: "There's something queer about this. What the devil do we want with loads and loads of baby food? That's about the sixtieth case of cornflakes I've seen." The relief thought for a few moments and then said: "I know as much about it as you do. But the last time we took a load like that on board we took evacuee kids over."

Even though Jack was not married—and had very little likelihood of being married—he had the strangest and the most touching regard for children. Children were very fond of him. And the thought of taking little children across the waste of the Western Ocean so terrified him that he didn't even tell his own mother and father the name of the ship that he was sailing on. He left his allotment note in the Board of Trade office, with instructions that it should be posted to them when the ship was out at sea.

The following night the ship sailed. They beat round the coast and early the next morning, at a secret rendezvous, they picked up the children. It was a strange and terrible sight to see them coming on board. They were all Scottish, with the most delicious accents. All frightened—yet trying to be so brave. When a man has seen cattle brought aboard, seen benzine pumped into a ship, and watched barges loading a ship with cordite, it may seem strange that the same man should have a feeling of sick horror when little children toil up a gangway carrying satchels, and with labels pinned to their coats.

They pushed off out to sea. And the children got so dreadfully sea-sick at first—then picked up so marvellously about four days out. The crew took them absolutely to their hearts. One little boy had to be begged, as a personal favour, by the four to eight watch of firemen, not to come down below into the stokehold, as the second engineer really didn't like it.

There was a little girl called Patsy, a blonde bombshell of about seven. The boys christened her doll "sticketh closer than a brother"—because Patsy would never leave the doll anywhere. And to see her pushing a minute perambulator, with an absolutely microscopic little doll in it, along the promenade deck—with her pigtails thumping between her shoulder blades—and her stumpy little legs, steadying her against the roll of the ship, was a sight to gladden the heart of any man.

The kids used to go up on the gun platform and gaze with awe and wonderment at Jack and the gun. And beg him to open the breach so that they could look up through the long, silvery rifling, at the blue sky. They were so pleased and so happy.

But at night—down below in the fo'castle—the sailors would look at each other, their eyes dark with bewilderment. They would make all sorts of plans for what they would do if a submarine did get the ship. "Now look here, Johnny. When the alarm hooters sound, you go straight to the after end of the starboard alleyway and get the kids out of the cabins and up on deck. And Bill—you take the forrard end, and don't forget all of you—those kids must be got safely into the boats. It doesn't matter a damn about anything else."

They wore their eyelids out looking for submarines. Frozen with cold, they stood watch and watch on the gun, and the lookout. There were always eyes gazing steadily at the water.

By the grace of God they got the ship safely into Montreal. They sailed up the St. Lawrence in the beautiful sunlight, and at night lights were lit on the deck. And children who, for a year almost, had known nothing but black-out, chattered excitedly and pointed to the river bank ablaze with lights.

They gave the children a most glorious and wonderful concert party the night before they docked. There was tea and cakes—and the cook worked himself into a muck sweat producing gallons and gallons of ice cream. A few little tummies were sick—but a lot of little hearts were made very happy. They gave a special show at the end of the concert, in which a sheet was hung up over the stage, and they played silhouettes. Dick, the enormously fat second deck steward—the children's favourite—was carried in groaning, laid on the table behind the sheet and they performed an "operation" on him. In the middle of a chorus of screams and howls from behind the curtain, a huge knife descended and, seemingly, cut his stomach open. Out of it was dragged yards and yards of sausages, tins of condensed milk, packets of cigarettes. The place rocked with laughter. But little Patsy, who was sitting on Jack's knee, started crying: "Oh, please Jack," she said, "don't let them hurt Dickie. Please don't let them hurt him."

They handed the children over the next day to the care of kind friends ashore. There were many tears, many kisses. Solemn handshakes from young gentlemen of eight—who had nearly split their fingers in two trying to splice ropes. Away they went. And the crew said to each other: "Boys, that's a good job well done. Let's go ashore and have a drink."

About a week later, in his cabin on the bridge, Captain Ashcroft—Jack's skipper—struggled to make a size fifteen and a half stiff collar meet round a sixteen-inch neck. With his head back, his face purple, he wrenched at the stud. Slowly his windpipe contracted, until he was in imminent danger of apoplexy. Then hole and stud met and the job was done. His braces hung down over his blue serge trousers—which were concertinaed over his shoes. On the bed lay his jacket, waistcoat, overcoat, and a bowler hat. As he tugged his tie into position he thought about his ship. As was his habit, he talked to himself. The steward and mess boy, washing dishes below in the pantry, could hear the dull rumble of his voice.

The boy, fishing about in the greasy water for the remaining spoons, grinned at his boss and whispered, "What's bit the old man? 'E seems to have a proper cob on this morning."

"He ain't got no cob," came the loyal answer. "What'd you do if you had one of them conferences to go to? They'll probably want to send us back in a seven-knot convoy, when the skipper knows she can do eleven."

The boy thought this over for a moment, as he swilled the water round and released the plug. "If we get's another seven-knot, then we won't be back for near a month. Mind you"—this with all the knowledge and depth of reasoning that characterises the first tripper—"I don't think she'll do eleven!"

The fat old steward put down his finished handful of spoons and looked at his young helper. "Well, I've seen some boys," he remarked, "I've trained some boys. But you beats the lot. You don't know port from starboard—can't even learn to set a bloody table—yet there you go, shooting out ideas. Man and boy I've sailed with Captain Ashcroft. I've been torpedoed with him twice in the last war, and bombed with him this war. If ever there's a man wot knows his own ship, how far and how ruddy fast she'll go, it's him!" He brought his clenched fist down to give the table a rousing thump, but changed his mind and tapped it with one sausage-like forefinger. "If he says this ship will get home in ten days, she'll get home in ten days! If he says she'll do eleven knots—" words failed him as he looked at the boy's stubborn face.

"Steward!" came a bellow from the cabin.

The steward gave his opposite number a withering look and turned about, round the alleyway, and up the staircase to the captain's day room.

Captain Ashcroft stood there, his face red with exertion, and a little purplish from the stiff collar. "Get me a clean handkerchief, George," he said, "and let me know when the launch comes alongside. Tell the senior sparks to be ready and—er—get me three glasses." George grinned, yet with all the loyalty of a man who has been a tried friend many years, "All right, skipper. Shall I tell chief to come up as well?"

"Yes, George," said the skipper, "get him up as well."

Ten minutes later three men stood in the day room. Charlie, the chief engineer—a tall man, weighed down with his responsibilities; a shock of light hair tousled over eyes that were blue and searching, yet with a lovely glint of humour; his six-foot of bone and muscle was draped over a chair back, his hands clasped a glass of rum, and his legs were spread apart. George, the steward—who wore a faded blue sweater and soiled grey trousers; short and fat, yet possessed an air of authority; a good man, beloved by all, and had started his sea career from a tiny village outside Whitby with the two men who stood there with him. And Captain Ashcroft himself who looked like a prosperous commercial traveller at first glance but, in reality, had master mariner written all over him. He stood there in his neat, blue suit, glass in hand, and he looked at his two friends. "I'm off to the conference," his voice rumbled out, "shall I get you anything ashore?"—Heads were shaken—"I should be back for tea, and I'm going to get my ship out of here by to-morrow morning if I've got to sail alone. It's got to be more than seven knots too. It's time we got home for a bit of leave!" Charlie shifted his weight, swallowed his rum, and murmured, "Off you go to town. But for God's sake don't promise to do over fourteen knots—the commodore'll get suspicious." The three of them grinned. And the skipper struggled into his overcoat as a voice came from below: "Launch alongside, sir," picked up his case and gloves. And, with a nod, went out.

Jack, leaning over the starboard rail, watched the launch speeding across the bay; then went below to join the boys in a game of poker.

The convoy conference room was a huge, vaulted chamber. In days of peace it was used as a banqueting hall, decorations of all sorts used to hang on the walls and ceilings, and the chatter of the town folk could be heard above the band, which used to play in the old minstrel gallery. Now, in the days of war, it was used for conferences; and there sat an old man. He was in uniform, the blue of a naval officer, a broad band around his sleeve, four ribbons of the last war glowed on his breast. He was the commodore of the convoy. After the last war he had spent a few more years at sea and then retired to lead the life he had promised himself. To wake up in the morning to his garden and his wife, nothing more exciting than to dole out mild and benevolent punishment to poachers. Never to sail again, unless in his own little fishing boat. When war was declared he was one of the first to offer his services, and now he shepherded unwieldy, lovable old tramps across the ocean.

Down in the harbour the sun shone clear. The ships lay at anchor. They looked a goodly company, and he recognised many old friends among them.

He rang the bell. "Tell the ships' masters that I'll be grateful if they'll come in at once," he said to the marine sentry. Then he lit a cigar and leaned back, waiting for them. As always, memories of past meetings filled his head. That dreadful meeting at the Admiralty—when they knew that they alone stood between their country and starvation. The long list of his friends who had died flashed across his mind. Good men and faithful—their ships staunch to the end. He shook himself out of his reverie—"We won the last war, we'll win this." He rose to his feet as the men came in.

First the captain of the port, his secretary, and then the masters. A few wore uniform, the rest lounge suits and their service badges.

There was Dutch Captain Bekker, immaculate in blue; escaped from the hell of Rotterdam, escaped to leave behind the bodies of his wife and family, and the ruins of his home; escaped from a living death, to continue a life tortured with hatred and heart-break. Old Captain Ashcroft sat there like a bull terrier. Ritchie, the captain of the Cunarder. Norwegian, Dutch, American, English. Forty-two men representing forty-two ships—under the guidance of one cunning old man. They sat there and waited for him to speak.

Papers were spread out, each sheet stamped "Secret." The port captain rose and read out instructions for leaving the port. As he turned each page there was a rustle, as forty-two other pages were turned. The port captain finished and sat down, and the com-modore rose. He had never overcome the initial nervousness of addressing people. He fumbled with his glasses, coughed looked under bent and bushy eyebrows at his audience, then commenced. "Well, gentlemen, this is my fourteenth convoy from this port. Ahem!—Let's hope it will be as successful as its forerunners." The class smiled dutifully. "Now, firstly, are all here quite convinced that an average speed of ten knots—ten knots, gentlemen—can be held?" All around the table heads nodded.

Captain Ashcroft sat there, his mind in a turmoil—his chin stuck out. "She'll do it," he thought. "She'll do it, I know. I'll get ten knots out of that ship if it kills me. It's damn silly to think of hanging around at seven knots. Damn it all, Charlie knows what speed she'll do! Why, that ship's been the pride of my heart, I know every move she makes. I'd be giving in to her to put in sev-en knots. Seven knots be damned. I've run messages for mother faster than seven knots."

The commodore continued: "You all know the danger that lurks for a ship that lags behind. We cannot stop for laggards. You all know your cargoes—this convoy must get through. We have excellent escort, and we hope, with God's help, to make the passage in fourteen days. In front of you are your instructions for convoy signals, a few codes of my own we can use in case of danger. See that your watch-keepers do not forget them. The last on the list, you will notice, is X.Y.Z. You will hoist this signal to denote 'disabled, I must drop astern.' The same Morse. I sincerely hope that none of us will have to use it." Then followed instructions about sighting the enemy, evasive tactics, smoke floats and all other details. The captains listened in perfect silence until the very end, when he concluded, "So that will be all. God grant we get home safely—as I know we will. And now there is a drink for each of you on the buffet. Let us drink to our *bon voyage*."

Chairs scraped back and there was a murmur of thanks as each man took his drink.

Captain Ashcroft stood there with a whisky in his hand; but his thoughts were away back on board his ship, down in the engine room with Charlie. Well, the die was cast. He would go back and tell them that, by hook or by crook, they would flog their ship and get her safely home in fourteen days. The lines on his face from nose to chin deepened, his glass was held as in a vice. He heard the commodore's voice: "Good luck, gentlemen." "Good ships, good seamanship," whispered the captain, and drank his tot.

The crew took the news very well. Charlie, the chief engineer, was worried; haunted the engine room—checking up on every possible thing. Then they sailed out, the whole convoy jostling and bucketing along, forming up in lines. She was a good old ship, had seen years and years of service, with quite respectable passenger accommodation. Used to do an intermediate run between Australia and China. She had been refitted for taking evacuee children. But now the bunks were empty, the blankets and sheets stowed away, the mattresses looking bare and uninviting in the cold rooms. The men felt the loss of the children keenly—the fo'castle seemed a dim and dreary place, the ship was very quiet.

Four-on and eight-off. And Jack held the four to eight. They ran into atrocious weather and the ship developed a shocking list.

A huge cargo of great steel barrels, full of petrol dope for high-powered engines, was securely lashed to the forrard well-deck. Under the pitiless driving of the engine the ship lumbered on, huge green seas engulfing her. She developed an indescribable roll. The men on the bridge gazed long and hard at the barrels, waiting for them—waiting for them to break loose. Then one night, five days from home a terrific, crashing green sea burst like a thunderclap over the fo'castle head. The entire fore part of the ship disappeared; hatches, winch, barrels, everything covered with tossing, foaming water. There was a dull boom as one of the barrels was torn loose and smashed back against the bridge. There was only one thing to do. Men worn out with lack of sleep, bodies racked with pain, looked at each other. There was only one thing to do; stop the ship, leave the convoy, re-lash the barrels, and hope for the best.

And they were in the danger area.

With a face like a mask, the skipper gave the curt order to the stand-by man on the bridge, "Hoist X.Y.Z." The man took the flags, each neatly rolled in its own separate compartment, clipped them together on the halliard and then hauled away. The scream-ing wind, like a solid wall, picked up the flags, whipping the rope almost out of his hands. The answer came back from the com-modore's ship, "Unavoidable, we cannot delay. Good luck." The steady beat of the engines, the life and heart of the ship, slowed like the pulse beat of a dying man. They slipped back past the whale factory ship, past the tankers, past the Cunarder. The escort astern hovered curiously around them. The sky grew dark, the wind rose, and the convoy went on.

That night Jack, and every available able-bodied man on the ship, went down to the bows. The barrels were in a state of chaos, jammed hard against bulkheads, upended. The acrid taste of lead seeped up. There was no steam on deck—the pipes had gone. Toiling, straining, sweating on the heaving deck—their fingers crushed and bleeding—their breath gasping out—the men strained and worked; their only respite to go back on the wheel and stand there while the sweat dried on their bodies. Their feet froze in their wet sea boots. Eight hours it took them, and when every barrel was lashed and secured the men staggered like drunkards across the deck. The bow dipped, and a huge roller— the father and mother of all rollers—smashed down. The little bunch of men was seized and hurled across the deck; icy, freezing water pouring into their clothes; smashed against winch and hatch top; shoulders and legs almost wrenched off. And the sea laughed, and rolled, and gurgled along the side as they picked themselves up. Two men, their heads covered with blood, their eyes blank with shock, were taken into the saloon and bandaged.

Jack went aft and sat down with his shipmates in the fo'castle. No use turning in, had to go on watch again in half an hour. He was shaken and frozen with cold; as he moved his toes the water in his sea boots squelched round his stockings. Stiffly he rose, peeled off his oilskins, took off his sea boots, and sat rubbing his aching, swollen feet; then bare footed, went to his bag and pulled out a clean pair of sea-boot stockings. Thick and long, of white, soft oiled wool, knitted by some dear soul for just such an occasion. With a sigh of relief he pulled them on. He took a dry cloth, tried to wipe out his sea boots, then went outside into the cold biting wind, and along to the galley. Good old Doc had done marvels with hot soup; standing there in his galley—a shambles of smashed gear, skylights battened down. Good old Doc, the most important man on the ship.

Jack took a little saucepan full of thick, creamy, boiling rabbit soup, and a huge hunk of bread. "Hey, Doc," he said, "we've got that deck cargo lashed up, but where the hell's the convoy now?" "Search me," was the answer. "We've missed it now. I suppose the next thing we get will be Mr. Bloody Focke-Wulf trying to lay his eggs down the funnel." Jack shrugged. There was the clang of eight bells and he went back on the poop.

They never caught the convoy up. They headed steadily eastward; the watches tightened up, men gazed constantly out and up; guns were oiled and cleaned, constantly loaded. The old ship shouldered her way on through the ocean.

They never caught the convoy up, but they got safely back to port with an extra lifeboat.

Some weeks later a sailor walked into a dockside pub. It was shabby, uninviting, and stinking of beer. The usual crowd of dockside workers, belated shipping clerks and others crowded round the long counter. At the back of the bar the wireless was faintly humming "Valse Triste"—it might just as well have been the fat stock prices for all the attention that was paid to it.

Then the door, held by a huge leathern strap, was pushed open and two men came in. The sailor, and a man who was an obvious clerk. The sailor was in oilskins and sea boots, a greasy uniform cap, with a faded badge, on the back of his head. In one hand he held a tiny suitcase, the type that costs about half a crown. Up at the bar the clerk said, "Will you have a glass of beer?" The sailor grunted. With the two glasses balanced on the palm of one hand the barman squirted the beer in, the foam rose and oozed over the top, and the beer was put on the counter. "And make it two double whiskies as well," said the sailor. The clerk looked a little peeved, fished around in his pocket book and grudgingly handed over a ten-shilling note. The sailor put his whisky down in one, then started to drink his beer. He seemed bored by his companion's chatter, and stood, with his elbows on the counter, contenting himself by watching the barmaid's every movement. She bridled under his glance—casting many skittish looks, of which he took no notice at all.

Finally the little clerk spoke up, in a rather peevish tone—"I don't know what's come over you, Jack. You come home, you stay two days, speak to no one, and then push off out to sea again. Why the devil can't you stay at home a bit longer? I could get you a job in the yard any time you wanted it—you'd be all right as a rigger, or a splicer. Yet here you are going off back to sea. Getting drunk. You've got no gear, and you won't tell anyone what's happened." The sailor said nothing. "Don't you ever realise anything?" continued the man. "Do you have to be a bloody fool all your life? Surely you've done enough for this war—why not stay at home and make a bit of money? I can't see any difference in the way we'll have to live—even if Hitler does win the war."

The sailor ordered another round. Then he turned, and holding the man's coat lapel between his finger and thumb: "Listen, you stinking little rat," he said. "If it wasn't for the fact that you're too small to hit, I'd push your face in. You won't understand it—you know nothing at all about it—but this is why I'm going back to sea. I owe this country nothing—I don't think I've had a particularly square deal off it. I went to sea this war because somebody had to do it—and I like Englishmen. … Coming back on my last trip, just about four days off Ireland, we sighted a ship's lifeboat. Well—the Germans have got a nice habit of hiding a submarine behind a lifeboat, so that when you go to pick it up—or examine it—you cross his sights at two thousand yards and he sticks a tin fish in you. Our skipper was in the last war and he knows a trick worth two of those. I'm the gunner, and I had orders to keep the gun on that boat the whole time. We kept our eyes peeled and got close to the boat. No submarine, no nothing—just sunset, nearly dark, a cold wind, and a ship's lifeboat bobbing on the water. We got alongside and all hands were called out. They got the derrick up, put steam on deck. And the boys went over the side—down the Jacob's ladder—fixed grapples—and the boat was hauled up. It was a tricky, rotten job. Just about getting dark, and the boat bobbing and rising on the swell—all hands dead tired and cursing the skipper like hell." He picked up his beer, drank it, wiped his mouth on the back of his sleeve and tugged the clerk's coat lapel a little closer. "When the boat was on the deck I went down from the gun to have a look at it. Couldn't see anything—no men—just a boat lying there on the deck, the steam puttering in the winches. I was tired and hungry and fed up. I saw a tarpaulin covering the bottom of the boat and I stepped on to it." Jack's face grew pale, the haggard look in his eyes deepened. "Jesus," he said, "I stepped into the boat, and I pulled back the tarpaulin. There were children there—children. Sixteen dead children. You could see the bruises and rings round their necks, where the life jackets had chafed them. You could see the look on their faces—and they were dead. Their hands had been cut and torn, their knees had been scraped as they tried to get into the boat. They had died of exposure—died on the Western Ocean without hope or help from God or man. If I'd ever been fool enough to get married they might have been my children, might have been the little boy or girl next door. They'd harmed no one. They were going to Montreal to get away from all this, to live their lives in decency and quiet, so that something might be saved from the bloody wreck that's been made of the world."

By now the sailor's hands were right round the lapel of the clerk's coat—his face was grey. "Do you realise that the Germans had waited for that ship—that they deliberately waited, and put a torpedo through her in the middle of a Western Ocean gale. I owe this country nothing. They sent me to a reformatory. They sent me to gaol. I never got any help from them. Two of my pals died at Dunkirk, another one's rotting his guts out in a German prison camp. When the *Courageous* went down I lost one of my best pals. I don't give one solitary goddamn for Democracy, or Fascism, or Communism, or Socialism. But when those Germans waited for those kids—when I helped to pick them up—this war became a personal matter for me. And now you want me to stay ashore. You're making a damned good thing out of this war, and you want me to join your ramp, eh? I wouldn't be seen dead in a ditch with you. Carry on, matey. You're giving no help, you're getting all the money—you're leaving it to bastards like me to fight your battles. Well, we will. And we'll win; we'll win in spite of you. And all those kids will be avenged." His voice had dropped to a whisper. The clerk was almost paralysed as Jack gave him one gentle, contemptuous push—picked up his little suitcase—and went through the door.

Ships sailed and convoys went through. The ships toiled over the waters, and all the refinements of modern warfare were inflicted on the sailors.

A man would say good-bye to his wife, pick up his bag and leave, and neither he nor she would ever know when he was returning. The dull crash of a torpedo, or the whistling scream of a dive-bomber would echo through their heads all day and all night. The man would be on look-out on the bridge, and it happened. Then, maybe months later, in the bow-wave of a ship going home—a sagging, sodden, pitiful body, held to the surface of the waters by a life-jacket—a reproach to God and man—would curl and roll past the ship. And the watchers would shiver.

Jack sailed. He came home for two or three days at a time, eaten up and burning with his own hatred. He cut out his drinking, cut out all thoughts of home and comfort—or marriage. He came home one time to find his street very quiet. Dick was dead. Jack's mother had kept the cutting for him, telling of the loss of another of His Majesty's mine-sweepers. Poor Dick. A life-time spent on the sea—and the sea had claimed him, as he always said it would. So, of the five boys, three remained. Tom was away God knows where—Harry and his brother Peter were bringing benzine back to England. Jack often thought of Harry—he thought of him every time he went for a drink and saw cars outside public houses. And he thought of him every time he saw army lorries, and heard tales from the drivers of taking two-ton lorries ten miles to buy gramophone records for the mess.

Jack signed on a ship. She was old; she was thirty years old. Rather like one of those comfortable old ladies one sees toddling up the street doing the morning shopping; very small and neat. And she, it turned out, was the happiest ship he had ever sailed on.

They went out forty odd ships, all plunging and bucking about the ocean. There were Chinese on deck, and below. White officers and engineers, two very young apprentices, two little sparks, and a ship's cat. They were bound for Takoradi in West Africa, and four days out the convoy was dive-bombed. Jack and the other gunners took their watches at the gun, engineers doubled up on watches below, the bridge never had less than four men on it. At night was heard the constant, thundering crash of depth charges.

And on those nights Jack, if he were on watch below, would race for the gun and stand in his position—waiting. And in the plume of the submarine he could see, not death for himself, but poor Joe—his face smothered with oil and grease, his body numbed with shock as he struggled frantically through the water— dragged down, in the end, to the death he had always feared. And in the plume he could see Dick—Dick standing smoking on the deck of a little mine-sweeper; on a smooth, calm sea. Then the crash of a mine—the blinding explosion—the steam; and Dick's mother sitting at home—calm, tearless, and waiting—waiting for the son who did not come back.

What did cold matter? What did privation, or hunger, or tired-ness matter? Who gave a damn about conditions at home or on ships? "Let's get them!" he thought. "It is not enough to be worthy of the dead. The dead must be avenged."

The convoy broke up, and alone the old ship beat her way down to the west coast.

Dawn broke over the waters; the sun showed as a thin gold-en line between the sea and the dark clouds of the trade winds. Slowly the sea grew brighter as the sky lightened; the deep pur-ple shadows in the trough of the swell eased up to blue. The air was warm and soft, and the light dew glistened on the winch. Rails were wet, silver globules dropping from them. Then the sun was up—and in the heavens the clouds sank back from menacing black banks of rain to light, frothy decorations on the horizon. The old tramp shouldered her way steadily through the water; a long wake, dead straight, leading away aft to the distant horizon.

There was a deep peace over all. The peace of an old ship that had battled her way across the waters in convoy and was now alone. For many days she had toiled along, nearly bursting her engines to keep up the speed set down. Men—tall, gaunt, hard—had stood their watch on the bridge and gun, and down in the engine room they had toiled and tended. Doubling up on watches; one man always at the controls—immovable, silent, strained—waiting for the harsh jangle of the bell that would warn them of imminent death; or maybe the horror of a lifetime with hideous scars from scalding steam or falling metal. With tender, frantic care the engineer would nurse his engines. Watching pumps, glands noting the steady feed of the oil; driving firemen to keep the head of steam that would urge the old ship forward.

Now all was over, the danger had passed. They were alone, and all hands went back to the blessed relief of four-on and eight-off. To sleep with the doors held wide open. To shave, to read books, to eat meals soberly and quietly; then, at the imperious yet friendly call of "One bell," to go back on watch.

The skipper thought of his ship and cargo. The mate left the bridge to the apprentice and wandered about in slippers and an old patrol jacket, checking up on jobs to be done on deck— "Winches to be greased and checked—starboard rail to be chipped and painted—give some white paint to the cook and get the galley clean—must see if the anchor cement has held under that last hammering." Round the ship he padded, pipe in his mouth, contentment in his heart. "Better get those boats examined and swing them back inboard on the chocks." Mist, white and comforting, curled up from the deck—with the promise of a warm day. "Flying-fish weather ahead," he mused, "we'll issue topees to-day."

In his cabin the gunner rolled over and sat up. The room, small, white painted, was spotlessly clean. Neatly folded on the deck were his trousers, shirt and coat. His shoes, black and glistening, the pride of Jack's heart, stood in trees beside them. Out of the bunk he swung; pushing his feet into slippers he stood up in his pyjama trousers, picked up soap and towel and stepped out on the verandah deck. The air was cool and fresh; he looked around happily at the far horizon and rejoiced. No convoy … no scars. There was the old four-inch, covered up. First thing he'd sponge her out. And the chamber had a spot of rust where the shell had seized a little—he'd get that off. Give her a good pull through, grease her, and then—a cloud hovered across his face. What was wrong with the training gear? Was it a jam? Had the race really broken, as he had dreaded? Why, the damn gun was so stiff that it would scarcely train on the beam. Still, he'd have a shot at it. Plenty of time to take the whole gun to pieces between now and Lagos. He strode to the bathroom, shut the door, slipped off his trousers, and filled his bucket. He picked up his huge sponge, dipped it in the water, then pressed it on his head just like Napoleon crowning himself. The tepid water trickled down his back, face and chest. His head was clear, tongue clean, and he felt happy. Through his teeth he whistled "Oh, Johnny!"

On the bridge the Chinese quartermaster struck eight bells as the head of the third mate appeared above the ladders. The mate was still on his rounds and the apprentice stalked the bridge in sole command. Spotless and white was his shirt, creased his trousers and shiny his shoes—marred by one black and one brown shoelace. His face pink and shiny, his white cap-cover a thing of beauty. Around his neck, dangling almost to his stomach, were the bridge binoculars. The third mate gazed ironically at him. "All correct, sir. Steering steadily. Eight bells. Now take those damned glasses off 'fore they break your bloody neck." The apprentice grinned sheepishly. The third watched the boy as he put the glasses back on the rack and went down the ladder. "How long is it," he mused, "since I did my first trip, when I had all my own gear brand new, and all brand new ideas? I used to have visions of a skipper's job, with all its ease and comfort; then I was ploughed by a God-forsaken little runt in a Board of Trade office—four years having my guts pulled out on a Whitby tramp at five pounds a month; just to be failed." Sadly he picked up the binoculars and had a look round. Nothing in sight. No sign of anything. Just the sea.

Later breakfast was served. Porridge, curry and rice, then bacon and eggs—and the off-watch men trooped in. Skipper, mate, second mate, chief engineer, second, fourth and the gunner. Talk was general.

Into the room stalked the ship's one and only passenger, Tims the cat. She—her sex was a mystery—walked sedately to the long settee that stretched the width of the saloon and leapt, with a soft plop, to the captain's side. Tims was a general—and a most impartial—favourite. Ten minutes before the gangway had been raised in Glasgow she had come aboard and adopted the ship. No one, not even the cook, could claim all her affection. She was seen amidships as often as in the quarters aft. Each morning she had breakfast in the saloon by the side of the skipper. Often the steward would present her with the menu, and her meals were eaten from her own plate. From thence she would do a full tour of the ship; stopping to gaze into the galley, peeping abstractedly into the rooms; walking delicately, like Agag, round the Chinese quarters. And from there to the poop, where she and the gunner would pace the narrow deck and wait for lunch. After lunch she proved herself a true sailor—she turned in to sleep, the sleep of the just, until eight bells; a saucer of milk awaited her in the chief engineer's room.

The old ship plodded gently on, her bow raining imperceptibly to the swell, the foremast tracing geometrical lines across the sky.

As the day wore on all the routine work on board ship was done. Rails were chipped, little white flakes of paint and rust powdering the deck. In the galley the acrid smell of paint fought the aroma of roast beef and baked potatoes. Down on the after deck chippy stood at his machine and put a razor edge on the knives of all who asked. The Chinese cook came from his galley and emptied a pan of boiled rice into a wicker basket; then, with bent back and elbows on knees, he shook it rhythmically up and down. The water, thick and white as milk, flowed out. He shuffled round and held it under the tap. The water gushed quicker, fading from its creamy white to a dull clarity. He shut the tap off, and stirred the rice with one hand as he watched the water drain into the scuppers. Back in Canton when the Japanese had infested the city, not even one grain of rice, not one drop of water would ever have been wasted. His mother, as she crouched over the cooking pot and doled out each meagre morsel of food, watched each grain— almost counted them. The starvation was so cruel that it was all a man could do to live and breathe. Yet on board this ship, with those greedy, wasteful, whining Shanghai men, how different.

"We do not like your cooking. Your chow is bad. Why do you not boil the eggs soft like the white people? We do not eat like the peasants or coolies. You are a worthless man."

Hard boiled eggs! As if any man did not know that they cling to the ribs, give a man feeling, strength, a great stomach. Yet they would finnick with soft food fit only for a child or a woman of the cities. So all his food, his labour, would be for nought. They would peer and pry into the bowls with poised chopsticks, eat what they fancied, throw away the rest. In Canton, under the heel of the oppressor, people starved. The very albatross that circled now above his head was better fed than his own family.

With a sigh he shuffled back into the galley, with the basket on his hip and a pain in his heart.

Jack had cleaned and prepared his gun. He'd have one last cigarette on the poop, he thought, and then turn in.

Damn good jobs these Chinese boats. Damn good. Better than running your legs off with a white crew. He took a last look round the horizon and appreciated its clean, bare line. The sun was about to go down in all its glory. Like darting arrows of light, the flying-fish sped over one wave to vanish into the next gently heaving swell. Little splashes of foam would appear as these, the most pursued of living creatures, escaped death in the air and the sea.

All over the ship work was laid down and men, pleasantly tired, turned their thoughts to food and small talk.

In his room, the apprentice, who had finished his meal, dragged from under the bed his portable gramophone and half a dozen scratched records. He would take his music out on the hatch top. The sky was a delicate, glowing pattern of colour; the sun had almost gone, and the sea matched the sky in all its changing moods. To the east, dark and mysterious. To the west, gold, black and purple. The albatross had gone; the waters creamed and kissed along the ship's side. In the ever-widening wake of the bow-wave dolphins, in trios, seemed to be drawn in beautiful arcs as they kept company. They were large, black, and somehow so very friendly, that the apprentice took out his favourite record and put it on the faded green turntable. It was "Missouri Waltz." The dolphins leapt and swayed to the music. Port and starboard they came up in their threes and kept tune—the gentle swish of their bodies forming a background of peace. The sun went down.

The old ship lumbered on, rejoicing in her heart with her crew. Thirty long years she had sailed. She had seen the skipper, now so great in his awful majesty, when he had first stepped aboard as a first trip midshipman. She had rung to his step as he stalked the bridge as master seventeen years later. Her engines responded only to the care of the chief engineer. She had watched him as he had schemed and plotted to get her repairs. Never once had she let him down—unless you counted the unfortunate affair of the whistle. She knew that chief and skipper would blow two blasts as they passed their houses on the Merseyside, knew as well as they did that two wives always waited. She hadn't wanted to let anyone down. But the frosts of Nova Scotia had cracked the joint; so that, when the cord was pulled, she had failed them. Instead of the two hoarse roars of welcome she had always given—the confounded whistle had broken off, nearly braining the bosun—a thin piping cckkk! like a rusty knife on a tin plate, had offended the ears of all hands. Gently the old tub rocked and swayed with silent laughter. The skipper had nearly burst a blood vessel and the chief had held his head in shame. Still, thirty years was a good record. A very good record.

The night drew the last vestige of colour from the sky. All was dark. Phosphorus gleamed in the wake of the ship, pale green; long, beautiful streaks of cold fire.

Suddenly from the starboard beam there shot a tremendous, great yellow flare—from the port bow the long, straight blobs of tracer bullets. "Good, this is it. Now is the chance," Jack thought, and hurled himself at the telephone. No sooner had he got the receiver to his ear than "Open fire"—in a calm, cool voice. "Good old MacGregor." He was at the gun, opened the breach and grabbed the rammer. Smack. His shoulders cracked under the effort as he rammed the shell home. Back to the canister, out with a charge, put it in, slip in a tube, slam the breach. The ship was being rent and torn with huge shells. The engines had stopped. The Chinese were flooding the deck, their bodies being smashed to a bloody gruel as they met the tearing shrapnel. It was hell. It was inferno. But, by God, he had a gun. Round to the trainer—his shoes split as he braced his feet to the deck and his shoulder to the barrel, and swung the wheel. Round she came. The cold, merciless eye of the searchlight came across his sights. Duck under the muzzle, set the range, bring her down. She's there, she's there, she's there ... and she's there. Pull the trigger. Crash went the gun; and the deck came up in a heave as the recoil gripped the straining girders of the ship. Had it hit? No matter—load again. Back aft for another shell. Then the world opened in one great blinding flash, his ear drums burst, and he was flung halfway across the deck. When he picked himself up the gun was lying on its side. Quick—up—along the poop—on to the well-deck—up the midship house. The bridge was alight. The ship was quaking, and rolling, and sinking. Jack had one thought in his head. "Let's get another shot at them—they won't get away with this!"

Then suddenly all was silent. And the captain's voice, "Abandon ship."

The extra fourth mate was signalling frantically with a little torch "Cease fire. Our boats have gone. Ship sinking." Silence. Then another murderous salvo of shells, from 2,000 yards range, smashed into the ship. Jack turned to go aft. He could hear the stammer of the machine-gun as the raider's supply ship raked them fore and aft. There was a sudden agonising crack and he fell forward on the deck—rolled over on his back—picked himself up—and took one stride forward. A grinding, tearing pain ran through his right leg. *"Jesus!"* he said. He held his leg up. There was a gruesome, nightmarish stump—and in the eye of the searchlight he could see the blood pouring out. He crawled to the starboard bunker hatch. There was old MacGregor, the chief officer—great big six-foot-four Mac—lying on his back on the deck. His clothes torn, his leg shattered, his shoulder broken and his spine hit. "Abandon ship. Abandon ship," came the steady voice. Then along came MacDavid, the second engineer. He seized MacGregor by both hands. Imagine the excruciating pain—to be dragged by the hands, with a shoulder torn by shrapnel. Not a word from MacGregor. Jack followed—sitting down. Dragging his shattered leg, pushing himself forward. On to the after deck, hopping down the ladder, and so to the rail. The raft was there, bobbing and bouncing on the water, held by a rope to the ship's side. There was an argument going on. Mac's voice came up—still calm, still steady. "I tell you it's O.K. You push me into the water, I'll get to the raft." With all those wounds, with all that pain, with his ship dying under him—and with his voice still calm and steady.

Mac went over. Jack stood up, leaned his belly over the rail, put his hands over and grabbed the lower bar. Pulled—harder, harder. His legs came down over and he fell with a splash into the water—down and down—his lungs were bursting. The water was green and cool, and bobbing up to the surface, holding his one leg stiff, he swam, and splashed, and reached the raft—dragged himself on—Bob Harvey, the second steward, was there—helping him, holding him. "Here you are, Jack."—He had a bottle of rum. The shattered end of Jack's leg hung in the water.

Others came on board. They could see the ship quaking, then they realised she was going down. Jack was roused from his daze. "The rope's still tied to the upper deck. Where's a knife?—quick—where's a knife?—where's the end?" They could see the stern sinking deeper in the water. Jack fumbled madly around his waist for his knife, his good sharp knife. Her stern was getting lower in the water and they could feel a gentle, remorseless tug on the raft. There was a slash as someone found a knife.

The raft broke free and the ship sank. She saw her skipper, with tears in his eyes, gazing at her in anguish. Water flooded her decks and holds. Oil, her life's blood, poured from one side—steam, her breath, gushed from the other. Still looking at her captain, she mounted high in the air, she bowed to the sky. Then with a roar, as of hatred and vengeance, she slipped under. The huge wave of her sinking rose and engulfed the survivors. The raft overturned.

There were sharks, and they knew there were sharks. Struggling madly they got back on board. One sound man first, then the wounded, then the others. There was silence, just the splashing of the water.

Then the eye of the searchlight swung over, picked them out, and a great burst of bullets was flung at them. An A.B. leapt to his feet screaming, and fell into the water. Another, clinging to a spar loosened his grip and sank. The survivors cowered as the bullets poured over them and into them. There were screams. Groans. Then the light went out, and the firing stopped.

Attacked, murdered, their ship smashed under them. Just sixteen men out of 83—and of those sixteen men three had been killed.

And the raft was left 800 miles from land.

All that night and all the next day—twelve hours in the night and twelve hours in the day—hours when the sharks came up from the depths of the ocean and made huge snaps at the men's legs as they hung over the crowded raft. Hours when the raft rocked and swayed—and the men knew that it was sinking. There was a man sitting by Jack on the raft—he never knew who it was—but that man kept his arm around him the whole time, preventing him from slipping off. There were consultations between the skipper and the chief engineer, and spark's whisper could be heard: "I think I got a message out." Mac lay in the bottom of the raft, his bridge binoculars still around his neck. The sun went down; the sharks that hovered under the water swept closer and closer. MacDavid tried valiantly to scare them away, smacking on the water with an oar. All hands knew that before the next morning they would be dead of exposure—or, if they were not, the raft would sink before the next night. Jack sat on the very edge of the raft with one leg tucked under him—bracing himself backwards—the end of his stump, gruesomely mottled with little jelly fish, dangled in the water. Then someone sighted a ship; and the sky was a flaming gold and red as the ship, an old Spanish tramp, came towards them.

And the midshipman, their little first trip midshipman, stood up on the raft, tied his soiled white shirt to an oar and waved it. And he blew on his little piping whistle—his cheeks distended— his eyes bulging with the fear that he would be neither seen nor heard.

One moment it seemed to Jack that the ship was miles away on the horizon and the next that it was almost alongside. The sharks circled constantly round the raft—the ship's propellers crashed constantly forward and astern to scare them off. Then the ship circled round, made a lee of dead water, and with consummate skill was brought along side.

Jack was weak—deathly weak—the strength had gone from his arms and his head. They lowered a huge fish basket, about six feet in diameter and five feet deep. He was lifted up, and with a despairing sort of gulp, threw himself forward to clutch the rim. He got it, he staggered, he almost fell. And then someone seized him by the seat of his trousers and flung him in. Strong, kind hands eased him out, and he was laid on deck in a blanket.

He knew by the jabber of tongues that he was on some sort of foreign ship. He was thirsty, his tongue was dry and swollen—a filthy, loathsome taste in his mouth. He tried to make signals to a man. "Water," he whispered, "water." And then, as the man gave him a look of blank incomprehension—"Water—eau." The man's big brown eyes widened. "Ah—si, si." He raced away, and came back with a jug—lifted Jack's head—and poured a huge mouthful of blazing, stinging, paralysing brandy down his throat. Jack's stomach writhed and his head seemed to burst open. His heart pounded somewhere up in his neck as he rolled back in the torment of that scalding, raw spirit. And then unconsciousness.

He came to lying on a bunk. The port hole was open, and outside the sea glimmered under the sky.

Jack was sick, very sick indeed. His leg seemed to have swollen, the gaping end had widened and turned black—the bleeding had ceased. He spent the next twelve hours between sleeping and waking, then delirium caught him. In one of his lucid moments the door opened and the captain came in. "There's a ship on the horizon, gunner," he said, "we think maybe it's that raider again. If it is, this captain is going to hide us. Don't worry, boy," And then unconsciousness again.

When Jack came to once more the room was full of men. Enormous great men in white, with great buff holsters and revolvers round their waists. He cringed back in his bunk, an expression of abject terror on his face. "My God," he thought, "it's the raider crew."

A man pushed forward and bent over him. He could see a sun-tanned face, young and rather good-looking. Clear, grey eyes. And the red and gold epaulettes of the Royal Navy. With a love, pity, and an understanding that none but a very sick man could ever appreciate, he got hold of Jack's arm, shook him ever so gently and, with a soft Canadian drawl, quietly murmured, "Now don't worry, Jack, you're all right. We're friends, Jack, we'll look after you. I'm going to put some morphia into you—send you to sleep." There was a faint little prick in his arm and all the grinding, seering pain seemed to go. They lifted him up, whisked him out, cut his tattered clothes from him, wrapped him in blankets and strapped him into a stretcher. They laid him on the deck in the shade and he looked about him drowsily.

Half a mile away he could see the great bulk of an armed merchant cruiser. MacGregor lay at his side, his eyes closed in sleep; his huge body securely strapped, his legs splinted and attended to. On guard over them where two stalwart men in the white of the Royal Navy.

Then something peculiar happened to Jack—something that he had never experienced before in all his life. He felt a peculiar, burning pain around his eyes, a constricted feeling in his chest, and something hot running down his face. He was crying.

He sobbed until the morphia took a grip of him. Then all his pain and suffering, all his hopes; his beliefs and his fears were hidden under a blanket of sleep.

Twelve hours later, on board the cruiser, they told him that his leg would have to be amputated just below the knee. He signed the little paper, written in such meticulous long hand; he asked the young apprentice to take a letter home to his mother—in case he did not recover. Then, with perfect faith and trust in the ultimate outcome, he was taken to the operating theatre. Morphia was administered by the chief petty officer and there, on a scrubbed table covered with a blanket, the young surgeon—steadying himself against the roll of the ship—performed a neat amputation.

Jack woke up the next morning in his bare little room and saw one foot. One left foot. And one hard, board imitation that deceived no one.

In five days they got to Freetown and he was sent to a hospital ship.

When a man has lived his life violently, driven his body to the utmost, when he has found that even the most extreme exhaustion can be rectified by twelve hours in bed—he finds it very hard to realise that he is a sick man. The appalling pain in his leg did not, strangely enough, worry him. But the curious inability to move his arms, the impossibility of sitting up, and the queer, rasping pain in his chest did worry him. He found out later that he was brought to the hospital ship with a gangrenous leg—despite the operation—double pneumonia, and weighing approximately six and a half stone.

One morning the padre came down to see him. A tall, heavily built young man, who asked him if he had been confirmed. He said yes, so the padre asked him to take Holy Communion—later he found that it was the Last Sacrament.

He took it and felt better for it.

After nearly five weeks, with many blood transfusions and constant attention from the nurses, he recovered from his wounds. The grinding pain in his amputated leg eased down to a dull throb. But he was still dreadfully weak. Each morning the flies would wake him up in a bed that was wet with sweat. As consciousness came back he relived all the details of his life. "Everything has to be paid for," he could hear his father say, "Mind you don't run up too big a bill for yourself." This, then, was the bill. He had been young and strong—could beat anyone his own weight and height. And now—that little mound under the sheet was his one leg. The arms that could lift weights and the fists that had flattened many a man were now like sticks; he, who could run up the ratlines, was now gasping for breath in an effort to sit up. He who had taken all he wanted, danced to every tune, dodged every issue, was finally caught—chained to a bed in a hospital—a cripple.

The bill was presented with a vengeance. He became very quiet. He was left alive on sufferance, he thought. Much better men had died, and even his vengeance was denied him. At times he contemplated suicide.

A thing that hurt him was the lack of exercise. Each day the sick-berth attendants used to go ashore, get a bus, and go to Lumley Beach to swim. When Jack was allowed to get up and given crutches, though he laughed and joked, it hurt him to see them going.

But one day strong hands carried him from the gangway and put him down in the stern of the launch.

It was heaven for him just to sit there, feeling the launch bounce along in the water and trailing his hands over the side. He was hauled up on to the jetty and stood up on one leg and two crutches, on dry land; into the bus with that happy crowd; right out ten miles, driven by a laughing black boy; and then the beach—long and gently sloped, palm trees almost to the water's edge, and the great Atlantic rollers thundering inshore.

He sat down and the boys got undressed, and ran to fling themselves through the rollers.

He felt again the deep, hungry longing to feel once more the use of his body. Big Jock ran towards him. "Come on, Jack," he said, "let's paddle your toes." Jack was lifted up and undressed—no costume needed—then, with his arms round two strong shoulders, he was carried down to the water's edge. He felt the water, felt its coolness on knee and thigh. He was delirious with joy. A huge wave slapped him in greeting. They braced him up, took him out further—past his waist—and then, "So long, Jack," they said, "don't try and swim back to England." They submerged like diving ducks and Jack went down into the green water, with his eyes open. He bobbed up to the surface and struck out. He could swim, he could swim. He could swim. Down into a dive, do a handstand—his ears were filled with the water's close silence. Then a few strokes and up to the surface, turning over. The sun beat down on him, filling him with warmth. The sea, his old friend, his tried and trusted friend, bore him up. Gently he rolled on the crest of the wave; Jock's mighty hands swept up, caught him, set him on his feet and they stood up gasping and laughing. Then Jack realised something. … He was standing up. He felt his soul singing with joy. And he knew then that he had nothing to fear. In the water with his friends—the sun shining down, the sand tickling his toes as the undercurrent sucked back—he regained himself. The boy from St. James's choir, the deck-boy who loved the sea, had survived.

The sun was setting when, tired and sticky with the warmth of the sea, they crawled back into the bus and raced back through the sunset, through the green fields and past the funny little native villages, to the jetty.

And Jack knew that whatever happened, wherever he went, whoever he met, he would never be quite so happy as he was on that day.

After that, life was easy on board and, except for having no news from home, he was quite happy.

Nurses, staff and doctors, padre, the boys, his fellow patients, were his very good friends. His leg ceased to bother him because he just wouldn't let it. He tried to imagine that it was just corns or chilblains that were hurting him. Above all, he refused to permit anyone to help him.

A month later he went over to another of the company's ships for the long voyage home. In the strict length of the articles he was Distressed British Seaman, entitled only to a third-class passage home. But he was among friends, men from the same company, and he was put into a first-class cabin. The ship was taking Australian fighter pilots and sergeant pilots to England, and he was made very welcome. They made it their job to ensure his safety if anything should hit the ship, make sure that he got into the lifeboat. It was good to be amongst friends like that. All hands combined to see that he was comfortable and well looked after, and when he expostulated they just said, "That's all right, son, you're one of us."

An Australian lady going to England to do war work also looked after him in every possible way.

Jack of course had lost all his possessions, and when the ship arrived at Glasgow he worried as to whether the emigration people would ask him endless questions, and keep him to the last. And then he would have to see about getting some money, try and get a taxi, get to a crowded station. The prospect was very worrying to a man as sick as he.

But the first man on board was the company's shore superintendent. He found Jack in the lounge and came up to him. "I've heard all about you, sonny. You go down to your room, and I'll bring the emigration people down to see you."

The super soon appeared, shepherding the officials before him. "This is one of our men," he said, "sailor who has lost everything. All his papers, and his leg. I want you to fix him up at once." They had him squared up in ten minutes, the superintendent gave him five pounds, sent a telegram—forty-two words of good cheer—to his mother, and told him to stay on board that night. Next morning he was sent by car to the station, with a steward to look after him; a carriage had been booked for him to travel in comfort; two special meals had been ordered.

He arrived in Liverpool and was met by another man who took him by car to his home—a distance of about fifteen miles. There had been some bad blitzing and, as he sat in the back of the little smooth-running car, his heart was torn with anxiety—for he had no news from home. "Oh God," he thought, "please don't let me go through this—please don't let me come home, after all this, to find them dead." They passed rows and rows of shattered houses, smashed offices. The car sped on as, with shaking hands, he lit one cigarette from another. They got to his own district and his heart was in his mouth. And finally the car turned into Jack's own street.

It was a bright and sunny day, the sky was a clear blue, and his own little street was still there. It was safe and intact. Each doorway held a neighbour, each neighbour was a friend. And there was his mother. She wasn't crying; he got out of the car, pulled his two crutches after him, swung himself to the pavement, hobbled over and kissed her. His face was grey and wasted; his body was thin and his useless leg dangled. But his mother seemed to notice none of that. She came over to him with her usual short, toddling steps. "Come on in, Jack," she said, "your tea is ready."

And he went into his own home, and had his tea.

The summer drew to a close and Jack stayed at home. With his kind old father's sympathy and understanding, and his mother's careful feeding, he increased in strength daily.

One day he met old Bill. Bill had given four sons to his country in this war and was left with a fishing boat, no one to help him, and a river full of fish. So Jack went out with Bill in the boat. It was such a relief to be sailing up and down the river, working, knowing that his body was getting stronger. The constant procession of ships soothed him, yet it irritated him—to watch them come in and to picture the men on board, or to see them outward bound in the bright face of danger.

In time he remembered fully the dreadful story of that night, the last night of his ship—and he would wonder if it were really true. One look at his shattered leg told him that it was. He had but to close his eyes to the sunlight and he saw the red tracer bullets, as they sped to the raft—the cold glare of the searchlight. He saw again his old ship, terrible and violent in her end, as she reared her bows to the sky and sped under the waves. How could such things be, how could they?

One day, over in Liverpool, while on one of his periodical visits to the Ministry of Pensions doctor, he opened his paper and read: "The ship was torpedoed … among those missing are:—

… H. Smith, second mate.

… P. Smith, apprentice."

Peter and Harry kept to the same ship. They had sailed out from London, and dodged trouble until they were loaded and coming back from Freetown. Just after four in the afternoon she was hit aft, wrecking the guns. The submarine surfaced, shelled them. In that inferno of shell and fire, and the imminent explosion of their cargo, the men slaved to lower the boats. Harry was just about to get into his boat when he thought of Peter—he had been on the four to eight. Through the smoke and over shattered bodies Harry forced his way aft to search the gun platform. No sign. Back along the deck, looking down the engine-room hatch—the great steel girders that had held the ship together against the pressure of all the ocean were twisted to the semblance of wet string. Into the shattered saloon where they had so often sat and yarned; looking into the wrecked rooms, with their decks ripped up by the force of the explosion. No sign of Peter. Up to the bridge, not noticing or caring about the dreadful list of the ship. … No Peter. He was turning to go when he saw someone in the chart room. He went in. Peter lay there on the deck, his head against the bulkhead. He was weeping. Harry dropped down by him, put one arm around him and eased him up. Peter looked at him in astonishment and joy; he stirred a little; he opened his mouth to speak; he gave a faint, whistling sigh and died. …

Harry sat there. For years he seemed to sit there. Peter looked so peaceful, so normal, but he was dead. The ship gave a lurch that threw them the length of the chart room. Harry picked himself up and, closing his eyes in the pain of that parting, he tried to pray. He could see St. James's Church in those dim, quiet days of his youth—when Peter, his mother and his dad sat in the front pew—when he sang in the choir. The words of a hymn came back deeply, poignantly to him. His mouth, parched and dry with shock, opened and all he could say, as the ship died with his brother was: "Oh God, our Help in Ages Past … Oh God, our Help. …"

Peter lay there so quiet, he leaned against the almost horizontal bulkhead. The ship trembled. "Oh God …" Harry peeled off his jacket, laid it over Peter's face, and went out. The boats seemed miles away. The ship was now on her beam ends. He walked down the port side into the water, his eyes glazed, his brain numbed. He struck out blindly for the boats. …

"The ship was torpedoed … among those missing are … H. Smith, second mate … P. Smith, apprentice."

So Harry and Peter had gone. "I suppose," Jack thought, "that when the bright little boys who have hidden themselves away in soft jobs, and the other fellows who refuse to earn more than about fourteen pounds ten a week because of income tax, I suppose that when they read that they merely close the paper and think, Oh well, just another ship gone—still we've got plenty more."

He felt impatient. Was there nothing he could do? Joe gone, Dick gone, Harry and Peter gone. To know that, to come back from the graves of brave men, and to see people wasting food. To remember those children. To remember the unbelievable heroism of tanker men—efforts frittered away by people who just didn't realise the enormity of the forces they were fighting. What was the use of the struggle?—Why carry on? Let the bastards stew in their own juices.

All day long his mood became worse. He visited all his old drinking haunts, and missed his last train home.

But that night there was a blitz. Great guns smashed their shells into the sky, planes droned overhead and there was the intermittent, shuddering impact of bombs. The streets were deserted and the sky was red with the light of fires.

He decided to spend the night in a public shelter—the tube station at Hamilton Square—on the platform.

And there his mood was changed.

The place had the queer stale smell of all underground railways. At each end was a black cavern, where the shining rails vanished into infinity. And he saw, in the dim glow of the electric light, that it was packed with people. Old men, a few young men, and an overwhelming majority of women and children. It was almost quiet—they were settling down for the night. They lay along the platforms, stretched out in lines eight and nine deep; an old blanket to lie on, a pillow or folded coat for their heads, and a blanket to cover them. The old men and women dozed fitfully against the wall; all the grief of mankind written across their faces, and in their tragic, toil-worn hands. Little children, their faces pink and their hair ruffled, lay by their mothers, asleep. Quietly, gently asleep. Women and children, wives and mothers, they lay there side by side, in haunting pathos.

But it was no scene of defeat. The homes they had cherished were down in dusty ruins, but they were there. The men they loved were away in some foreign land, or the encompassing oceans bearing them as they sped with food and aid for Britain. But they were there. And as he looked the scene seemed to spread out, the vaulted roof seemed to part and vanish, to let in a great light that shone down on the people of Hamilton Square. And not only Hamilton Square, but every square in every city of this land. And not only this land, but every other land where humble, harmless people were holding up the tenets of this, our civilisation. Here was the whole civilised world. Here was victory.

Jack walked along, his crutches making little sound on the wooden floor. Up came the shelter marshal, very old and kindly, and his eyes red rimmed with exhaustion. "Missed the train, sonny?" he whispered. "Come along and I'll get you a bunk—we've got some spares."

They walked along. A woman feeding a baby at her breast looked up, smiled, and wished them goodnight. Two fat old ladies with shawls over their heads and arms comfortably clasped over capacious bosoms, smiled gently at Jack and one asked him in a hoarse whisper: "What's happened to you, lad?" "I got a packet at sea, ma." Their faces grew grave, and the other said: "God bless you, son. Look after yourself."

Along they went. Further on a little supper party was being held; tea; sandwiches, and a bag of meat pies. They looked up as Jack passed, a little boy gazing in wide-eyed wonderment. He heard a pattering of feet behind them and, turning round, he saw the small boy, who gasped, "Please, ma says would you like a cup of tea?" The marshal smiled and said: "You go ahead, I'll be fixing a bunk for you."

He went back to the party, and he sat down by the little boy. They were so very decent, offering him their tea and their food, and they behaved like old friends. He told them of the ship, they talked of the blitz and their homes that had been smashed; the little boy leaned more against Jack, and when he looked down, the little fellow was asleep. He left, and they all settled down for a night's rest.

Steering carefully along the narrow ledge, all that was left of a platform ten yards in width, he made his way to his bed. He was very tired.

Under one of the lights, in the middle of that throng, there was a woman—forty-five or somewhere near it. By her side, asleep, were two little girls and a small boy. She was crying. And some-how Jack felt impelled to stop and talk to her.

"What's wrong?" he said, as he sat down beside her. She looked at her children, and then said: "I've had no news from my hus-band at sea for eight months." She looked at Jack's leg and his crutches. "What's happened to you?" "Oh, nothing," he said. "I'm a sailor, and I lost this at sea. Is there anything I can do to help? I'm always meeting the boys, and I'll try to get some news for you." "Thank you very much," she said. "Before this war start-ed, you know, when he sailed out I could always get the 'Journal of Commerce' and look the ship up. I could see where he was, and think, 'Well, he's getting into Cape Town to-morrow, so he'll be back in two months.' Then I'd feel happier, because two months is not so long to wait. And there were always letters. Me and Mrs. Johnson, that's her over there, used to go down to the Allotment Office every Friday; or one of us would go down and leave the other to mind the children; we could always get news. Then this war started. I know Bill could get any job he wanted ashore—rigging; but when they've been to sea so long it seems such a rotten trick to leave just because there's danger. Bill got torpedoed and came home, but he's in such a temper over seeing such a lovely ship go down—it was her maiden voyage—that he signs on a troop carrier with Mrs. Johnson's husband. We can't stop them. I was just crying when I thought of the last time I saw him. I gave him his favourite supper—he likes a bit of fish, a nice fish steak with some potatoes and sauce. Then at ten o'clock he gets up, and we went upstairs to where the kids were asleep. Johnny there is his pet. Then we goes downstairs, and he just looks at me and says, 'Cheer up, Edna Parsons'—he always used to call me by my maiden name—it sounded so funny. 'Cheer up,' he said, 'I'll do a short trip and I'll be back. So when you hear two short hoots on the whistle and a long one, go out and buy me a bottle of Guinness.' Then he went out—that was eight months ago. The house has been blown down but we're safe. Just to do my bit and get even with the Huns, I got a job in an arms factory; mother looks after the kids all day. We're all friends here, and I don't do so bad." Her face lit up. "Won't he be pleased," she said, "I've put down my name and been accepted for one of the new tenement flats. When I get the time I'll move in—he won't half be surprised. And I've saved twenty pounds from his allotment." Her voice died away as her memories came back.

"Bill's right, you know," Jack said slowly. "When you've been to sea all your life it gets you. I met three men who had been forty-three days in an open boat; they were in hospital with me in Freetown. One came back to Liverpool a month before me—yet, when I went to see him, his wife told me that he had been back at sea for a week. I suppose there's quite a lot of men going to come back home, as your Bill will, to find the home's been blitzed—the furniture gone—but you here. Yet Bill will go back to sea as soon as he can. He won't even bother to look for a shoreside job. Haven't you ever wondered why?" She looked at Jack, puzzled, a tired woman of middle age. "I do wonder," she said. "I always think I want him to get a shore job, but with this war on I don't think I'd like him to do it." "I think that's the point," said Jack. "We can go to sea and take all the Germans can give us, and expect all this when we get back. But as long as we come back and see our wives, or mothers, or sweet-hearts carrying on, then we'll do the same. If you ever decided to pack in, if you ever thought the game wasn't worth the candle, so would Bill. And so would everyone. But so long as you go on, setting him your own example, then there's no power on this earth that'd stop him from sailing. Keep your chin up, and remember you're an important person to us all; so look after yourself. Keep smiling, and Bill will be drinking that Guinness with you sooner than you think." He put his hand on her shoulder as he raised himself up. "Could you give me some sort of an address, and I'll see if I can get some news of the ship for you?" She smiled up at him happily. "You see that," she said, pointing up to the huge white and blue enamel sign—HAMILTON

SQUARE. "Well, my name is Edna Brown. Until I get the flat my address is right here, underneath the Ham of Hamilton Square."

"Goodnight to you, Missus." "Goodnight, son," she said. "God bless you."

He walked away, picking a path over the prostrate bodies, down the platform to where the old shelter marshal stood. Then he looked back, but Mrs. Brown was not to be recognised in the distance.

The marshal led Jack to a little bunk in an alcove; he had even produced a mattress and two blankets from somewhere. But Jack couldn't sleep, he lay awake thinking.

With all the strength, and life, and endurance that was left in England—why had not someone arisen to tell the world of the struggles of the little peoples of the earth? Why did not someone tell the world at its fireside the story of the heroism of these people? And the sea, the stories of the sea. Who would ever tell the story of old bosun? Who would ever tell of the reformatory, that dreadful institution, with the pitiful waste of lives and happiness? And who would ever tell the story of Dick and Joe, of Harry and Peter Smith, and of Mrs. Brown; of the struggle—silent, unending and bitter—of the powers of darkness to crush and subdue? Why not weld these people into one solid mass, one great fist that would smash the great monster of oppression and tyranny that had arisen before them?

So, with a brain very tired, Jack fell asleep.

The next morning he awoke to find the people had vanished like a morning mist. Not a sign, not a scrap of refuse or anything remained. He had a cup of tea with the marshal and took the next train home.

That day the weather changed and it was bitterly cold. He fell to thinking of Tom and Betty. Where was old Tom? In war-time you never could tell where a man with a gun ticket would be. He decided to look Betty up and get news from her.

He got over to town and went up to the little pub where Tom and he, Dick, Joe and Harry, and all the rest of that good company used to meet and drink. He had a drink, a lonely, quiet drink, then went outside. He propped himself up against a lamp-post to wait for a tram, watching people pass. ...

Two feet. Just to have two feet, to look down and see two shoes, just think of it; not having to take the bottom of your trouser leg, fold it up and pin it somewhere under your knee. God, it was horrible to get out of bed, or even just to wake up and see those two crutches constantly before you, propped up against the wall. Never to be able to see yourself in a mirror unless they were there under your armpits.

Looks so easy to walk, doesn't it? You merely raise one foot, swing it forward—you can feel your heel touch the ground, feel the spring of your instep, feel your toes curl over slightly—then the other foot comes forward and you can feel your hips working.

And to sit down in front of the wireless when they are playing that beautiful lilting music. Remember being with your girl when you bought that record of Duke Ellington playing "Mood Indigo;" and she came home with you, and you danced? You were a good dancer too, and the girls gave you that appraising look when you went up to ask them. Remember that girl in the Liverpool dance hall—she looked so beautiful, so sort of aristocratic, and that wonderful, smashing gown she had on—she sat back with a faint look of patrician disdain on her face. You straightened your tie and pulled your jacket down, shot your cuffs out looked to see if the trouser crease was all right; walked over to her and, with the slightest and most formal bow—in the very best Marie Corelli manner—"May I have the pleasure of the next dance?" you said. And she answered in the accents of Paddy's Market, lemon women, and all the slums of beautiful Liverpool, "Sorry mate, I'm took." That was funny!

Remember those warm summer days, with the smell of sea water and the air alive with heat. The band playing at the crowded bathing pool. Nothing on but a pair of shorts. Your body glistening, and rippling with muscle. You climb slowly and easily to the very top of the thirty-foot diving platform, go to the edge and look over, with your hands on your knees. See your girl and wave to her. Back to the end of the platform; a deep breath, three long bounding steps, up, throw yourself forward landing on your toes. Every muscle works as you hurl yourself forward into mid-air; waist flexible, knees stiff, toes pointed, whipping down to a perfect jack knife. Then straighten out and you go whistling down, and the water hits you—stings and burns around the sunburn. You shoot up to the surface, and strike out with an easy crawl stroke to the side. You come out like a porpoise, pulling yourself over the side in one long, easy movement. And walk over to your girl, running with water and brushing your hair back with both hands.

The tram came along and Jack got on board. Right up and out of the town, back to the little avenue. Slowly up the road, resting for a few minutes—he had never realised before how long the road was. There was the gate and there was the number—"Oh God, I hope Tom's safe."—He rang the front door bell.

Betty answered the door, her eyes quite blank and unrecognising. He said, "Hullo, Betty, where's Tom?" Then he noticed the look of horror on her face, the rings round her eyes, and that she was wearing black. "Come inside, Jack," she said.

They went into the little living room; in the corner was a cot, with a baby asleep. He sat down heavily. "What's happened?" Poor Betty. Poor quiet, grave, harmless little Betty. "Betty, tell me what's happened?"—He could see her eyes getting red, see the two little trickles of tears running down her face; see her hands knotting and unknotting. "Betty, darling, tell me what's happened?" "There's very little to tell—ship was torpedoed—four survivors.

A fireman, the deck boy, the carpenter's mate and the galley boy. All the reports are different—all they know is she was hit by a torpedo—I've had news of his being presumed dead. I have to go out to work."

"How old is … ?" he said. "Little Tom," she said. "Thirteen months. What happened to you?" "I got a packet off Freetown. I'll be getting a cork leg soon." "Oh Jack, you do look so ill, can I make you a cup of tea?" "Thank you."

The baby wakened and stared, the living image of Tom. Betty went over to him and lifted him out of his cot, looked at him and kissed him. Jack held his arms open. She put the baby into his lap and went out. He could hear her sobbing quietly and deeply, and he sat there with the baby in his arms. Little Tom. So all that was left now was one-legged Jack and little Tom.

They had tea in dreadful, frozen, constrained silence. A gentle, hurrying patter of rain on the windows; a tiny room; Betty and little Tom, and Jack; and sorrow.

So they were torpedoed and Tom was gone. Gone after a lifetime on the sea—gone, if it comes to that, with thirteen pounds ten given to his widow for the clothes he lost. Lying at the bottom of the ocean, drowned like a rat, while men at home slacked when they should have built more escort ships—played cards when they should have made guns. Tom had never slacked. He'd worked, he'd brought food home.

Jack went home. The tramcar was alive with noise, and empty of people. Clashing and banging, it clattered down the road. And he sat there with his crutches in his arm and thought—while anger rose up inside him. Anger and hatred. "Joe and Dick, Harry and Tom—and me left. Joe and Dick, Harry and Tom; good, clean-living men—dead. And me left. I'd have done better if I'd been sent to Dartmoor. I'd have had my two goddamn feet." He sat there with his crutches in his arm.

Next morning the wind was cold and bitter, the sea was grey. Jack went out for a drink, went back for his lunch, went out to the pictures, then went home again and sat before the fire, brooding. The war had taken him, lifted him, made him, and then shattered him. With a feeling of bewilderment he stared at the two crutches leaning against the wall. "What did you say, mother, about a reporter?" His mother stirred and opened her eyes. "He's calling back to-night."

That night the man did call back. Small, dark; with neither a particular accent nor mannerism. The mother left them alone.

"You're Jack, aren't you?"—as they sat together in the dim little room—"My name's Desfarges—I'm from the B.B.C. I heard over in Liverpool that you might have a story to tell."

Jack looked up from the fire. Looked at him, into him and through him. Then he picked up a pile of more than a hundred neatly written pages headed: "LOG BOOK—by Jack Fisher."

Two hours later a dazed, rather emotional gentleman of the B.B.C. left the front door of number fifty-seven. Jack slumped in the doorway and watched him disappear down the street towards the river, and into the night.

Why did I tell him about the raft? Why did I tell him about the raft? Why did I tell him about that bloody raft?

"What d'you mean, 'story to tell?' What story? Story of when I was up the Yang-tse fighting the Japs for two years? Story of when I was with Potato Jones running in and out of Alicante? You want stories? Listen—I'll tell you stories."

Easy. Dead easy. Just get to a microphone and talk.

From his heart, from the depths of his soul, a voice—"You bloody liar! What do you know about the Yang-tse—you don't even know how to spell it! Have you really forgotten where you spent your twenty-first birthday? Let me remind you—you were in borstal. You were a dirty little sneak thief—remember? The Spanish War! All you know of Spain is onions! Listen, Jack, remember how you always said the B.B.C. was punk. Now's your chance—it's here— it's waiting. It's going to happen. Put it over—you'll have the Air."

Oh God, why did I tell him about that bloody raft?

"If it's a good story there may be a fiver in it for you."

A good story. Christ, a good story! So that's what they think it is. After all I've been through—the hours on watch—that ghastly raft. Being with the boys on the *Silver Foam*—and then to hear of them dying one by one on each trip home. To be left. And the B.B.C. might think it's a good STORY.

TALK BY SEAMAN GUNNER JACK FISHER:

I'm Jack Fisher. I live at No. 57, Fisherman Street, Wallasey, Cheshire. You don't know me—you never will know me—I'm one of the bad boys. Once I was twenty and full of life and hope, yet your system sent me to a reformatory. What good did that do me, what good did that do my immortal soul?—to mix with gangsters, to learn all about sodomy, to learn the ins and outs and best ways of getting a prostitute to keep you. You spent eighty pounds a year, dear little tax-payers, to keep me there. And when I came out you spent your time and energy in keeping me from a job. And then, my sweet readers of schedule "A," I pushed off back to sea. I've lived amongst lice and filth. I've come back after a long trip and had to burn every stitch of my gear because my mother doesn't like bugs in her house. And yet I was happy and contented. I had my friends; and somewhere in the back of my mind I had the feeling, dear listeners, that at least you would leave me alone long enough to find some sweet girl, and court her, and get engaged to her, and marry her. All I wanted was three pounds a week. I was prepared to work till the sweat ran out of my ears to get even that. You didn't care whether I loved music, you didn't care whether I liked reading decent books. You said to hell with my aspirations. And when I got drunk and behaved like a university undergraduate on boat race night, I was slung back into gaol. But when the war started you forgot all about that. It was "Arise, British sailors, sail out and bring back our food for us. Don't mind the torpedoes, or the dive-bombers, or the raiders. Please feed us." Okay, we did. I did, and Tom, and Dick, Harry and, Joe. My friends are dead—they died for you. And it may interest you to know that I'm sitting here now with a funny little, grotesque stump where a perfectly good right foot used to be. I owe you nothing, but it's quite obvious that you owe me a lot in happiness and dreams. Yet I tried to save a ship for you—we all did. The people to whom you lent money after the last war, the gang you watched build itself into a nation—the gang I saw practising in Spain—the nation of beer drinkers machined-gunned me and my mates on a raft. It was left to an old Spanish tramp steamer—itself risking death—using the seamanship you never even admitted, to rescue us. And now I'm back home. You've done very well by me, I must admit. I have no cause for complaint. A pension of thirty shillings a week while I'm incapable and thirteen shillings and fourpence for two years as long as I can stand on two legs—one of them a wooden one—meets with your full approval, doesn't it? But it doesn't matter, DEAR PEOPLE, I know the country I'm fighting for. I know the liberties we want to preserve. I and the rest of the bad boys—the men of the depression—the men of Dunkirk, and of Crete, and of Greece—the boys who've sweated their hearts out in Libya—and the men who go down to the sea in ships. We'll fight your war for you. We'll win it. But, my God, there'll be some interesting little ceremonies afterwards. We'll win the peace. Goodnight.

Why did I tell him about the raft?

"I'll see you in Liverpool. Know that little café in Cases Street? Right—I'll arrange for the recording car to be there at four."

Jack went back into the room, closed the door, and sat on in front of the fire. Jack, cold and tired. Jack, with one leg. Jack, dead. Jack, crucifying himself.

All the misery he felt, all the frustration poured like a poison into his brain. When the time came for his bed he was shaking with venom and fury. His dreams that night were full of horror, his waking moments full of loneliness.

Next morning the wind had died down, the river was a flat and peaceful calm. Jack had his breakfast, went down and sat on the promenade and watched the ships, his beloved ships, sailing out. The thoughts that had stewed in his brain all night were gradually taking shape. A message—his justification, his revenge.

After a quiet bit of lunch with his mother he went off to the ferry and made his way over the waters. He sat down on top of the boat; he could see the man at the wheel, the officer on look-out; see the sunken ships in the harbour, the shattered buildings on either side. He was feeling rather ill and very weak. He lit a cigarette and sat back in the wintry sunlight—his thoughts miles away, thinking of the friends who had gone and the men he had known.

Looking over the side into the muddy water, his gaze seemed to travel thousands and thousands of miles to some deep, dark ocean. Floating in the water was a little, dark body; it seemed to rise, floating gently to the surface, the clothes ballooning grotesquely about it. The head held back, water streaming through eyes and nose and ears; a great jagged gash in the side showed how death had come. Around the waist was still strapped the leather cartridge belt and rammer of No. 2 breach worker on a four-inch gun.

The figure was revolving slowly in the water. Up, and up, and up. And then Jack saw that it was Tom. Tom lay on the water looking up at him, his face unmasked. "Have you forgotten about me so soon, Jack? I didn't ask much of life either, you know. I loved my wife. I've only seen my little son twice, yet I'm here and my wife is lonely. Did I die in vain, did I die unnoticed even by you? There are other people in the world like me, Jack, who deserve a lot more recognition than you'll get. Put me on your ship, Jack. Tell the world how I died—please don't leave me. Remember I was your friend. Put me on your ship."

Then Joe came up. Poor Joe; poor silent, stubborn Joe. Still in the uniform of the Royal Navy; still with that look of surprise that he had worn when the torpedo hit the ship and he had died. "And what about me, Jack? I had a sort of education. I wanted to be a doctor, you know. The country didn't do so well by me, yet I never complained. I spent all my life in fishing boats—in cold, wet, dreary weather. I never had more than ten bob to spend in my life. I, too, wanted a house, a wife, and children. I might have had them if it wasn't for this war. But I'm not complaining. Remember how we used to sing together in the choir?—remember that time the old organist played Handel's Largo and we both cried? Don't be bitter, Jack. Remember me."

Then Dick. His face still had that broad, cheery grin. "What's gone wrong with you, Jack? You weren't like this on the old *Silver Foam*. Look, we're passing her old anchorage now. We never expected much from life. But do you remember those Sunday mornings when you'd call round for me after breakfast and we'd walk along the prom laughing and joking; and then go into the local for our beer? I died to preserve that sort of thing, Jack. I died and my mother's still grieving. I can hear my wife crying every night. Don't try and kid yourself that you went into this war from bitterness or boredom. You went in for the same reason as I did—to fight for the little, decent things in life. What you say to-day may be heard all over the world. Remember your pals, won't you? Don't let us down—don't let yourself down."

Jack got up and slowly made his way to the stern end of boat. It isn't fair, he thought. Why should I remember? I've got my own life to live—I was never allowed to live it. Every man for himself.

The twin propellers of the ferry boat curdled the water into a long, creaming wake. The sun shone down, and Jack propped his knee against the rail and leaned over. A picture of the old lady of Las Palmas flashed across his mind—with the piece of meat in her hand as she almost ran away from the ship. She turned back and her ghost came walking towards him across the water. "Don't do that, Jack," she said. "Once, I know, you were a good kind-hearted boy—with your funny little dreams. Don't be poisoned. Remember us—you can give us peace—you can tell the world nicely. It's always the poor that help the poor. Once you gave me meat. And now, for the sake of the others, can I ask you for your brain and your help?" And she leaned down and kissed him.

With the four ghosts standing around him, Jack gazed on into the water.

An unbearable struggle was going on in his head as the little boat tied up at the pier. With his crutches under his arms he walked ashore. Men and women that he had seen, and known, and worked with followed him through the streets in a silent, invisible horde. Their voices rang in his ears. He could see the dreadful wounds many of them carried; memories of the last dreadful hours spent in suffering and pain. Tom, Dick, Joe and Harry headed the long procession that seemed to fill the whole street. They blocked the pavement, they seemed to stop the traffic. Trams and cars went right through their ghostly bodies. But they were there and they were real; the hard core of the resistance, of the decency of mankind.

Along the streets he went and he was pursued. His shoulders ached as he tried to make his crutches work faster, faster and faster—to propel him out of the reach of those clutching hands.

"Hey, you! Boy!" A sudden command made Jack stop and turn. There was bosun, his first bosun, the man who had died on Jack's first trip. Still dressed in his faded dungarees, the bald patch on his head glistening with sweat, face red and a two weeks' stubble on his chin. "And what do you think you're going to do now? You make me sick! I saw you come aboard for your first trip. I kicked your arse around the ship and you deserved it. I should kick you around the street now because I know—I know, boy—what you're going to do." His huge hairy paw shot out and he held Jack by the shoulder. His deep green-grey eyes bored through him. He took a deep breath and emphasised each remark with a tapping finger on Jack's chest. "So you're going to be the sailor. The sailor! I've wrung more water out of me sea-boot stockings than you've ever sailed on. So you've been keeping a Log Book, have you? I've seen some of your entries. 'Three years at borstal'—making yourself the poor little victim! Why didn't you tell the truth about being sent there? Remember the woman who was sorry for you with your bloody vacuum cleaner and invited you to her house? You stole her ring. You stole it, took it over to Liverpool, and kicked yourself when you could only get ten bob on it! You were pulled in, taken to court and put on probation. You should have been horsewhipped! and you didn't even have the sense to keep your dates with the probation officer. He might have done you some good, but you never gave him a chance. You never gave even your mother and father a chance. You lied to them. Lied. And lied. And lied. Then you stole again. Remember what your father said in court? 'My wife and I have no control over the boy. We can no longer be responsible for him.' That's why you went to borstal. Don't try whitewash with me, boy. I know you. Two years on a sailor's Gethsemane. Two years as a trimmer. Sailor's Gethsemane! Sailor's Gethsemane my arse. Two months with double rations on a sailor's paradise you mean. You never really went to sea. A few trips satisfied you, then get your pay-off and poodlefake ashore. You were lazy, you were a lazy little bastard. You could never stand the work, you never gave things a chance. And now you're going to tell the world that you've done trip for trip with the bosun. How you fired your little gun all on your own. You little bloody hero!" His voice dropped. "Listen now, boy, I liked you once. You had the makings of a good sailor. You love the sea and you know sailors. We can't speak—those of us left alive are almost speechless. So listen again, boy. You go to this machine. You tell 'em you're a sailor. But tell 'em about us—all of us. Tell 'em not about how you fired your gun—though you can do that—but tell 'em about the time when you were on that raft. How you cried. Cried like a baby the only time any one really hurt you. Tell 'em how your shipmates behaved. Put Tom, who was a real sailor, on your ship. And Betty, who's a real sailor's wife, mention her. Do it, boy. Do it for us, the forgotten men—and we'll forgive the rest. Good luck." He squeezed Jack's arm and stepped back into the crowd.

A great peace entered into him. He felt free. All the doubts and the indecisions, all the fears and bitterness that had haunted him, and twisted and tormented, were gone. His course was perfectly clear. He felt his soul singing inside him—a complete, wonderful confidence.

He smiled happily and turned in at the doorway of the little café.

It was quiet and dark—a long, shadowy counter—and at the back a little alcove. He sat down at a table.

Dick sat himself at the table, and Tom, and Joe, and Harry. All of them were in the room as Desfarges came in with a microphone, and a little Scotsman. The microphone was rigged and Desfarges said: "Go ahead when you like, Jack. Say what you want, say it how you please. Speak the truth of what you know." He went out. The little Scotsman took out his watch and spoke into the mike: "Okay, recording car. We're going ahead in ten seconds from … from now."

Tom leaned forward: "I'll be on your ship, Jack." Betty leaned forward: "I'll be your girl." Dick just looked and smiled, and "lovely grub" was all he said. Joe said, "Thank you, Jack." Harry held his arm. Old bosun gazed steadily at him.

And there amongst his friends—his wounds forgotten, his bitterness gone, and with the knowledge of the ultimate truth and the final good of what he was doing—Jack took a deep breath and began, slowly and quietly, with. Infinite humility: "I'm an Englishman, a sailor, and my first name is Jack. I'm quite an ordinary sort of individual, all we sailors are. We have a job to do and we do it. …"

THE END

FRANK LASKIER 1912–1949

Printed in Great Britain
by Amazon

82561312R00059